SET IN STYLE

THE JEWELRY OF
VAN CLEEF & ARPELS

Lattice bracelet owned by H.S.H.
Princess Grace of Monaco. Paris, France,
ca. 1935. Diamonds, platinum. Private
Collection of Her Serene Highness
Princess Grace of Monaco, Principality
of Monaco

SET IN STYLE

THE JEWELRY OF
VAN CLEEF & ARPELS

SARAH D. COFFIN

with contributions by
SUZY MENKES
RUTH PELTASON

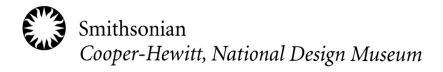

Smithsonian
Cooper-Hewitt, National Design Museum

NEW YORK

CONTENTS

6   FOREWORD
Bill Moggridge, Director,
Caroline Baumann, Associate Director,
Cooper-Hewitt, National Design Museum,
Smithsonian Institution

10   INNOVATION
Sarah D. Coffin

70   TRANSFORMATIONS
Sarah D. Coffin

110   NATURE AS INSPIRATION
Sarah D. Coffin

148   EXOTICISM
Sarah D. Coffin

190   FASHION AND
VAN CLEEF & ARPELS
Suzy Menkes

228   BEJEWELED LIVES
Ruth Peltason

280   NOTES

282   SELECTED BIBLIOGRAPHY

284   SELECTED INDEX

286   ACKNOWLEDGMENTS AND
PHOTOGRAPHIC CREDITS

Drops pair of earrings. New York, NY, ca.
1975. Platinum, diamonds. Courtesy of a
California Collection

Bill Moggridge, Director,
Caroline Baumann, Associate Director,
Cooper-Hewitt, National Design Museum

FOREWORD

Nécessaire. Paris, France, 1928.
Gold, blue, black, and white enamel,
sculpted lapis lazuli, rose-cut and
baguette-cut diamonds. Van Cleef &
Arpels' Collection

Amethyst, diamond, emerald, jade, onyx, ruby, and sapphire—the very
words conjure up an exotic world of beauty, fashion, mystery, and
intrigue. *Set in Style: The Jewelry of Van Cleef & Arpels* provides ample
evidence that the celebrated jeweler does indeed exemplify that world.
Van Cleef & Arpels has proven to be an innovative design leader for
over a full century, and with its ability to transform itself and advance
the traditions of jewelry making, VC&A is adding to its traditions in the
twenty-first century.

Marriage brought the Arpels and Van Cleef families together in 1896,
leading to the formal foundation of the jewelry business ten years
later. They developed a name for quality in fine traditional pieces in
the next years, adding dramatic new designs for long necklaces and
dangling earrings to suit the flapper styles of the 1920s. Dresses in
the 1930s returned to more flowing, feminine lines, accompanied by
wavy hairstyles, cigarettes in long holders, and miniature boxes for
accessories. Van Cleef & Arpels was quick to design these containers
as well as the necklaces and bracelets that complemented the clothes.
Headquartered in Paris, long a center of creative design for fashion and
jewelry, the company expanded its reach by adding a New York location
for the 1939 World's Fair, later adding a design and development team
to create designs specifically for the burgeoning leaders, aristocrats,

heiresses, and industrialists of North America. Renowned for its wonderfully stylized renditions of themes from nature, the firm also created mosaics of gemstones that became known as "Mystery Settings." Their clips of birds on a branch, flaming torches, and dancing ballerinas were inspired statements of love and hope amidst the perturbation of the Second World War. In the 1950s, VC&A's popular jewelry, especially its designs for the American market, mirrored the sweet romance and optimism of the postwar era. As Suzy Menkes says in her essay, "The correlation between fashion and jewelry is above all about a feeling, a sensibility, and an emotional grasp of the decorative arts in ever-changing times, and throughout its long history, VC&A has understood that link." In another essay in this catalogue, Ruth Peltason's "Bejeweled Lives," we learn about the seemingly endless stream of stars and dignitaries who have adorned themselves or their loved ones with designs from Van Cleef & Arpels, from Marlene Dietrich, Greta Garbo, and Elizabeth Taylor to the Duchess of Windsor, First Lady Jacqueline Kennedy, and Princess Grace of Monaco.

For *Set in Style*, we are most grateful to trustee Esme Usdan for her leadership of the Museum's Exhibitions Committee and for originating the idea of organizing an exhibition on Van Cleef & Arpels, as well as to Sarah Coffin, Head of the Product Design and Decorative Arts department at Cooper-Hewitt, National Design Museum, who selected nearly 350 masterpieces by Van Cleef & Arpels, many of which were created exclusively for the American market. In the four essays she has written for this publication, she examines VC&A's numerous achievements in jewelry design and reveals many fascinating stories behind the firm's iconic designs.

Very special thanks are also due to Van Cleef & Arpels, especially Stanislas de Quercize, VC&A's President and CEO, and Nicolas Bos, VC&A's President and CEO for the Americas and Worldwide Creative Director, for their partnership on this wonderful project. When we approached them with the idea of this exhibition, they, along with Kristina Buckley, Vice President of Communications, Nicolas Luchsinger, Director of the Heritage Collection, and Catherine Cariou, Museum and Heritage Curator, marshaled their forces on two continents to allow us access to the best objects in the firm's history and the never-before-published treasures in their archives. Thanks to their efforts, we offer in this exhibition and book an unprecedented amount of curatorial research. We also express our sincere appreciation to the many private lenders across the globe who have made it possible for us to assemble this unmatched and stunning display of historic and contemporary jewelry innovation. Lastly, we would like to thank Apple, which has generously loaned iPads to help us present these objects and enrich our visitors' experience in truly forward-thinking ways.

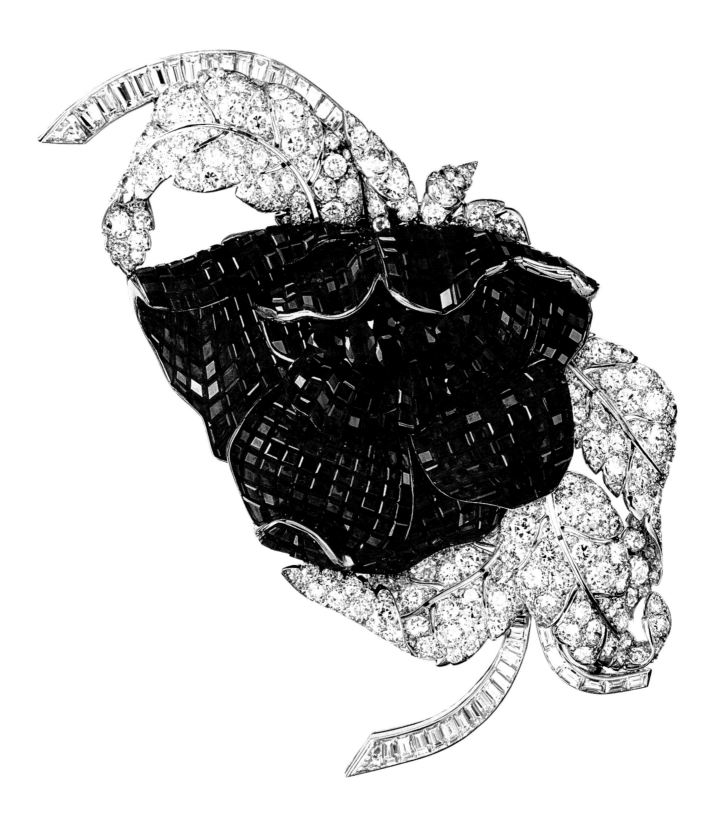

By Sarah D. Coffin

INNOVATION

For jewelry enthusiasts around the world, the words "Van Cleef & Arpels" summon up images of glamorous gems and personalities, fashionable boutiques and addresses. But what makes the firm important from a design perspective? In a word: Innovation. Fashionable figures come and go, but Van Cleef & Arpels has sustained a continuous focus on high-quality materials, workmanship, and design. Its desire to maintain an overarching vision through artistic direction and a commitment to innovation, combined with a keen sense of marketing, has resulted in a distinctive aesthetic that has influenced consumer taste over more than a century.

While VC&A was founded in Paris, American style and taste have played a major role in its history. Right from the beginning, in 1906, Americans were VC&A clients; the archives indicate pieces destined for them well before the existence of a permanent location in the United States. VC&A's initial attempt to establish a boutique in New York was thwarted when the stock market crashed the day the New York branch opened in 1929. The 1939 World's Fair brought the firm as exhibitors to New York, and a New York store opened after the close of the fair in 1940. New York was and remains the only location other than Paris with its own design and production capabilities.

Special commissions have made up an important part of VC&A's design history from the earliest days, often combining the imagination (and sometimes gemstones) of the client with that of the designer. In fact, the earliest known extant object is neither jewelry nor for a French client, but an American one (fig. 1). It is a bell push presumably made for an extremely wealthy American, Eugene Higgins, in the form of his yacht, *Varuna*.¹ Made of semi-precious and precious stones with sophisticated enameling, this minutely detailed model of Higgins's yacht on a sea of choppy-waved jasper required artisans acquainted with age-old techniques of enameling and stone carving. A barely visible gemstone

Mystery-Set Peony brooch. Paris, France, 1937. Gold, platinum, diamonds, rubies. Van Cleef & Arpels' Collection

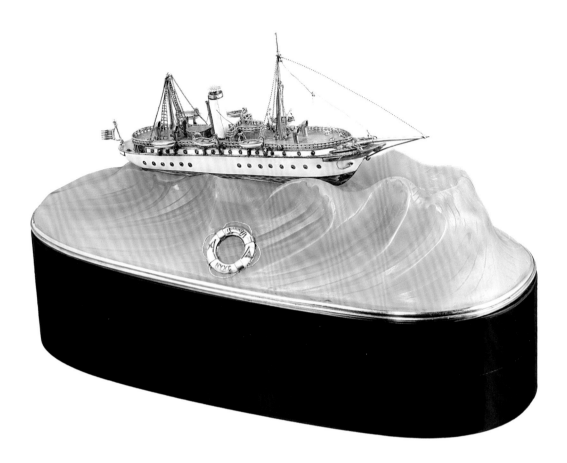

Fig. 1. *Varuna* bell push. Paris, France, ca. 1908. Yellow gold, silver, ebony, enamel, jasper. Van Cleef & Arpels' Collection

button, almost lost in the sea of virtuosity, recalls its function: ring for the butler. Its technical qualities call to mind the best eighteenth- and nineteenth-century objects of vertu (fig. 2), whose primary impact was to display virtuosic craftsmanship and design but which had an ostensible function, such as a snuffbox.

The combination of these skills with goldsmithing to create works had been centered in Paris in the eighteenth century, but by the time this oversized bell push was produced, Karl Fabergé from Russia reigned as one of the top purveyors of precious objects to Russian and foreign clients. Fabergé's work was also the rage at the 1900 *Exposition Universelle* in Paris, possibly providing a source of inspiration for the creation of this model. In the 1900 Paris exhibition, Fabergé, Louis Comfort Tiffany, René Lalique, and numerous other creators of luxury objects presented richly worked creations, some in the style that came to be known as Art Nouveau after Samuel Bing's pavilion "de l'art nouveau" at that exhibition.

Paris at the turn of the twentieth century was an international capital of fashion, design, and retailing, a must-see-and-be-seen destination for those able to afford it. Russian nobility and aristocracy, whose first language was usually French; American Gilded Age millionaires eager to show they were as sophisticated as their European counterparts; Indian Maharajahs enthusiastically adopting Western society— the cosmopolitan elite came from around the world to see and buy in the latest of style. It was in this Paris that

Fig. 2. Snuffbox. Switzerland, ca.
1785. Gold, enamel. Cooper-Hewitt,
National Design Museum, Smithsonian
Institution, Gift of Anonymous Donor,
1967-48-2

VC&A was founded in 1906 and soon opened its doors at 22, place Vendôme, not far from Lalique and the Ritz Hotel. While the founders, Alfred van Cleef and his sister Estelle and brother-in-law Charles Arpels, never espoused the Art Nouveau aesthetic, they saw the potential market for high-quality handcraftsmanship combined with the use of precious materials that designers like Fabergé and Lalique presented at the Paris exhibition. The success of this production, a natural fit with the Van Cleef and Arpels families' backgrounds in the diamond and gemstone business, provided the initial impetus for the firm's direction. Their aim was to emphasize fine, cut stones as part of the identity of their jewelry. Moreover, the color and use of these stones had a symbolic function influenced by the Symbolist movement, as embodied by the paintings of Odilon Redon.

Top jewelers may buy or be asked to use extremely rare and valuable gems as pieces by their most illustrious clients. However, when the stone is truly magnificent, less is often better, and creating a design that supports and enhances a star stone can be a difficult design assignment. Although VC&A has handled many major historic stones, it has established its reputation by designing pieces that feature the artistic design while coordinating elements such as the specific qualities and color of stones to maximize the potential of the stones and other materials. The design and production process ranges from stone and cut selection, which emphasizes the jeweler's skills, to an understanding of the broader context of the artistry and design, which is the purview of the artistic director or designer.

VC&A designers have always shown an affinity for restrained, abstract, geometric designs. They quickly saw the appeal of the sharp-edged, prismatic look of faceted cut stones and their connection to certain artistic movements of the day, such as Cubism, codified in Guillaume Apollinaire's 1912 work *The Beginnings of Cubism*.[2] This led the firm to a design in an avant-garde style now called the Deco style (fig. 3). But well before that, VC&A's background and aesthetics stood in contrast to the multimedia and metalwork background that produced René Lalique and Louis Comfort Tiffany, who had helped create the success in Paris and elsewhere of Art Nouveau and mixed-media creations.

The 1925 Paris *Exposition des Arts Décoratifs et Industriels Modernes,* the exhibition from which the term Art Deco comes, was originally planned for 1916 as a dissenting reaction to the excesses of Art Nouveau. World War I intervened; it is impossible to know how different the 1916 show would have been from what actually was displayed in 1925, but at the very least, some elements of the Deco style might have become codified earlier. Even without an exhibition, the forces of modernism combined with the technological advances and shunning of superfluity during World War I to encourage more restrained styles.

VC&A came of age in the 1910s and early 1920s and clearly allied itself with the abstracting and geometrical tendencies of the nascent Art Deco aesthetic. It produced what could be called Art Deco jewelry well before the 1925 exhibition. In fact, the lambrequin brooch of 1919 (fig. 4) is a stylistic leader. While a great deal of VC&A's artistic heritage was built on emulating nature and the imaginary, a spirit of abstraction has also dominated the firm's work throughout its history. Thus, an arrow becomes more a play of geometric shapes than an object shot from Cupid's bow in a 1918 hat pin (fig. 5).

Fig. 3. Pendant necklace. Paris, France, 1925. Platinum, pearl, diamonds. Courtesy of Private Collection

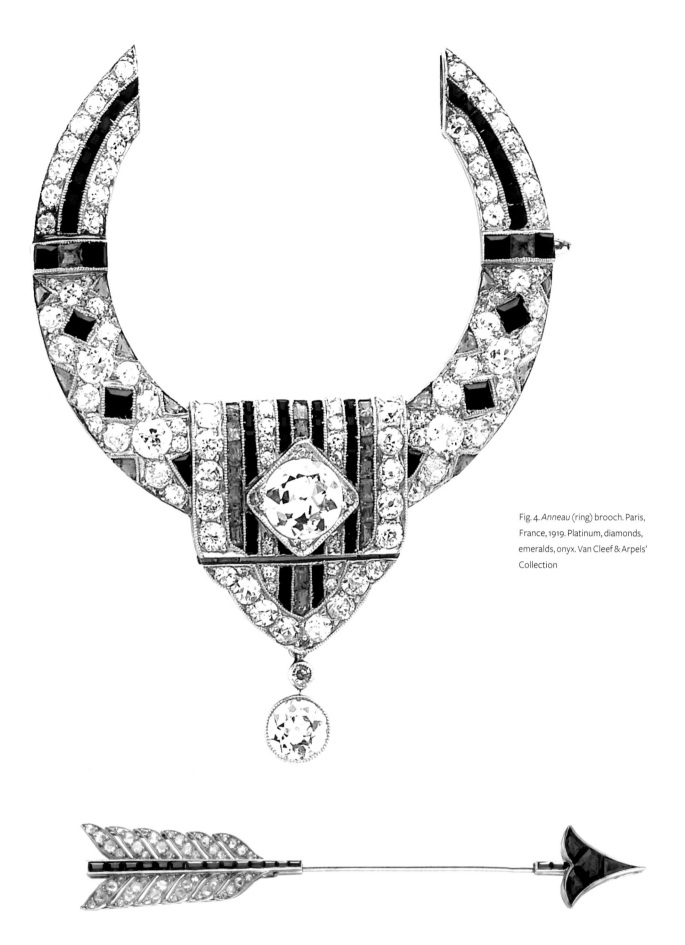

Fig. 4. *Anneau* (ring) brooch. Paris, France, 1919. Platinum, diamonds, emeralds, onyx. Van Cleef & Arpels' Collection

Fig. 5. Arrow hat pin. Paris, France, 1918. Platinum, diamonds, sapphires. Van Cleef & Arpels' Collection

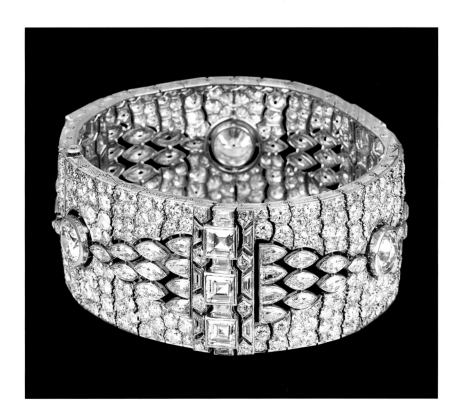

The concept of making connections between the fine and decorative arts was virtually nonexistent in the nineteenth century, but it took a significant turn early in the twentieth with the crossover work of the Wiener Werkstätte and in the world of dance, especially the Ballets Russes and the artists who contributed to its designs. In art, it was the works of Colorist-Orfist artists such as Sonia Delaunay—the subject of a major exhibition and book at Cooper-Hewitt, National Design Museum on view concurrently with this one—who transposed the color conversations from the paintings she and her husband Robert Delaunay created to the world of textile design. In Paris of the 1910s and 1920s, the force of Cubism and other artistic movements led designers to connect decorative arts, jewelry, and theatrical design with these and other fine-arts movements, such as de Stijl in the Netherlands. A late 1920s photograph entitled *Poème* depicts the interconnectedness of the time: a model is seated wearing a dress by French couturier Jean Patou and VC&A jewelry, in an interior by Jules Leleu, a major Art Deco designer whose work was featured in the 1925 Paris exhibition.

Women enjoyed more freedoms than ever in 1920s Paris, and VC&A responded with new object and jewelry designs that showed an innovative move toward larger and heavier pieces that continued into the 1930s (figs. 6, 7). Some jewelry shared with the decorative arts an interest in fine and exotic materials. Jean-Jacques Ruhlmann's rosewood furniture, Jean-Michel Frank's shagreen and leather furniture, and Jean Dunand's lacquer (see Exoticism, p. 158), lacquered metals, and jewelry all were among the works presented at the 1925 *Exposition Internationale des Arts Décoratifs*. The VC&A works reproduced in the French section of the catalogue include a châtelaine watch of onyx, sapphires, and engraved emeralds somewhat similar to one in the VC&A collection (fig. 8); and a black

enamel, jade, diamond, and amethyst *nécessaire*, a type of travel kit, with a three-tiered fountain on a column of jade with cascades of water in diamonds, both of which spoke to exoticism, above a bracelet whose diamonds were set in large links of rectangular and circular shapes in an entirely new aesthetic very close to Cubism.[3] Despite the emphasis on abstract geometrization so prevalent at the exhibition and of which VC&A was a leading practitioner, the judges awarded the Grand Prix to a bracelet set with stylized roses in a Chinese-inspired arrangement. However, this innovative bracelet is a well-integrated composition, mixing Chinese inspiration based on nature into a new style that would become nature-based Art Deco. A nécessaire of the following year (figs. 9,10) uses the same motifs in an even more Deco style than the winning bracelet. Inside this gold and enamel box with ruby and emerald flowers, the necessities of an evening out can be hidden away. While the milieu might have changed from the eighteenth century, the name and its essential purpose, a luxurious accessory that held a woman's "kit" for an evening out, remained the same. The VC&A archives show that the box design was "chosen by Mr Van Cleef" and ordered in July 1925 from Strauss, Allard, Meyer,[4] which produced a number of precious objects for VC&A and a few other important firms in the mid- to late 1920s. The nécessaire was also very much of its own day, as some Deco-style pieces made then show (fig. 11).

An eighteenth-century woman of a certain social standing was seldom without her ivory dance card in an appropriate box, her beauty patch in another (fig. 12), or her box of snuff, a form of powdered tobacco. The woman of the 1920s engendered fads for objects derived from those of her eighteenth-century forebear. The snuff box turned into the cigarette box (fig. 13); and the cigarette lighter might double as a lipstick holder (fig. 14). Indeed, when used by women, snuff and cigarettes both had the same slightly risqué connotation. VC&A went to great lengths to produce objects of equal or greater luxury to their eighteenth-century counterparts, without referencing old designs. Châtelaines, a form much featured by VC&A in the 1920s, trace their roots to the eighteenth century, when elaborate brooch-like objects, in gold and other media, had chains from which pendant watches and other "necessities" could be suspended, and were generally worn by men. VC&A updated the concept to be a dress accessory for women. Their efforts led to some of the most sophisticated designs, workmanship, and innovation ever created by the firm. These elegantly hidden watches helped the owner take a surreptitious glance at the time, which would have been considered a social faux pas if done too visibly.

Fig. 8. Châtelaine watch. Paris, France, 1924. Platinum, sapphires, diamonds, onyx, enamel, pearl. Van Cleef & Arpels' Collection

Fig. 8. Châtelaine watch (detail)

Fig. 9. Nécessaire. Paris, France, 1926.
Gold, mauve jade, rubies, enamel,
sapphires, emeralds, diamonds. Van
Cleef & Arpels' Collection

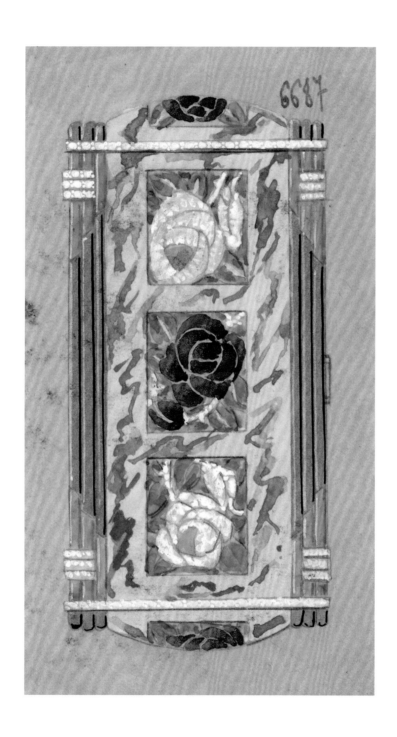

6687

Fig. 10. Retail stock book showing
nécessaire 6687. Paris, France, 1925.
Gouache on paper. Van Cleef & Arpels'
Archives

Fig. 12. Etui. France or England, ca. 1750. Shagreen (shark or ray skin), gilded copper, gold. Cooper-Hewitt, National Design Museum, Smithsonian Institution, Bequest of Sarah Cooper Hewitt, 1931-6-104 and NA 1012a/g

Fig. 11. Nécessaire. Paris, France, 1925. Yellow gold, blue enamel, cabochon sapphires, rose-cut diamonds. Van Cleef & Arpels' Collection

Fig. 13. Cigarette case. Paris, France, 1962. Yellow gold, cabochon sapphire. Van Cleef & Arpels' Collection

Fig. 14. Cigarette lighter clock. Paris, France, 1936. Styptor, gold. Van Cleef & Arpels' Collection

Fig. 15. *Nécessaire design no. 26536*
retail card. Paris, France, 1925. Pigment
and ink on card. Van Cleef & Arpels'
Archives

In this spirit is a vanity ordered in 1925 and completed in 1926. The lid's design and
execution are by Vladimir Makovsky (1884–1966), a Russian émigré artist-designer from
a family of talented painters in Russia. His talents for composition also included an ability
to design in marquetry of mother-of-pearl and hardstones (figs. 15, 16). Produced at
the workshop of Strauss, Allard, Meyer, which also created the Chinese-inspired box
mentioned above, the box illustrates the degree of detail that went into these works,
referencing earlier boxes by French, Swiss, and Russian makers (fig. 17). Makovsky's work
became known in New York not only through VC&A but also because Black, Starr, and
Frost, direct American rivals to Tiffany &Co., also had a Paris presence and commissioned
the designer to work on some inlaid clocks for sale in the United States. While much
of Makovsky's work shows the influence of his travels in Asia, this vanity has a distinctly
medieval subject. Its theme was not an obvious choice for the Art Deco show, but it was
lauded for its suggestion of French medieval design as a source of inspiration by the
chauvinistic promoters of French design production.[5] The equation with the bestower's
chivalry would not have gone unnoticed to the user.

Some of VC&A's most beautiful boxes were ordered up in 1927 from a *boîtier*, or box
specialist, named Alfred Langlois. He produced both the highly sophisticated enamel
decoration in Chinese taste and the model of the box with a Persian carpet–like design;
along with a nécessaire of more abstract Deco design with carpet-like rectangles
and diamond ice pyramids, predominantly in enamel (fig. 18). Initially, Langlois was an
independent master of a workshop, soon expanding his repertoire for VC&A from boxes,

Fig. 16. Nécessaire. Paris, France, 1925.
Yellow gold, enamel, mother of pearl,
rose-cut diamonds. Van Cleef & Arpels'
Collection

Fig. 17. Snuff box. France, 1858. Gold, enamel. Cooper-Hewitt, National Design Museum, Smithsonian Institution, Gift from the Thomas W. Evans Collection from University of Pennsylvania School of Dental Medicine, 1983-69-15

often jeweled, to VC&A's most detailed and exacting pieces of jewelry. By 1932, Langlois worked exclusively for VC&A. He continued as a principal jeweler for the firm until VC&A acquired his studio much later.

VC&A cultivated similar relationships with top-level watchmakers, who provided exceptional enamel work, gold engraving, and gem settings from their watch-making tradition. It sought out technical and beautiful solutions that hid or revealed their secrets in unique ways, and always with the eye of a jeweler. The firm rightly saw the potential of timekeeping combined with fine jewelry to create precious objects from night clocks to watches (fig. 19). When platinum, a stronger, more expensive alternative to silver, became more widely available after World War I, VC&A was among the leading jewelers to successfully employ it for jewelry mountings. It enabled the designers to make a clean, linear mounting that was lighter than gold or silver, allowing the refractive powers of the stones to shine through without the risk of tarnish to clothing (fig. 20).

While the 1930s witnessed economic depression on a global scale, a market for luxury jewelry remained, albeit on a limited scale, demanding new designs and new materials to excite consumers. VC&A produced some of its most innovative designs during the pre–World War II period, such as the Minaudière, a cross between a clutch bag and a large nécessaire. According to legend, it was designed for Florence Jay Gould, a notable patron of the arts and one of many personalities who embraced VC&A jewelry and objects (see Peltason, p. 248). The result was a feminine case for feminine things, such as a compact, lipstick, comb, and mirror, but also a few other additions, such as a calling- or dance-card holder, pill box, a space for money or a handkerchief, a cigarette case (often with a lighter on the side), and a hidden clock. This way, the not-always-acceptable habit of a woman smoking could be concealed yet accessible, and one could check the time via a sliding door or push button.

Fig. 18. Nécessaire. Paris, France, 1928. Gold, blue, black, and white enamel, sculpted lapis lazuli, rose-cut and baguette-cut diamonds. Van Cleef & Arpels' Collection

VAN CLEEF & ARPELS

DIM 6 AVR

Fig. 19. Pocket Chronometer with
Calendar timepiece. Paris, France,
1926. Platinum. Van Cleef & Arpels'
Collection

The object and name Minaudière (based on the verb *minauder*, meaning to use affected manners, such as fluttering) were patented in 1930 in affectionate honor of Estelle van Cleef, who was said to have charming social "minauderies." It was a feat both from a design and technical perspective to fit all of these well-made objects into a portable, jewel box–like clutch, often set with a jeweled clasp and sometimes held in a satin frame (fig. 21).

Among VC&A's numerous technical successes in jewelry, the most significant achievement remains the *Serti mystérieux*, or "Mystery Setting." First used for a Minaudière and patented in 1933 (fig. 22), this technique features stones grooved to set into T-rail channels made of gold, which is more supple than platinum. A marvel of design and technique, the setting was at first only viable on the flat surfaces of boxes and then

Fig. 20. Bow brooch. Paris, France, 1928.
Platinum, diamonds. Van Cleef & Arpels'
Collection

Fig. 21. Minaudière. Paris, France, 1934.
Yellow gold, emeralds, diamonds
(case); satin. Van Cleef & Arpels'
Collection

flat sections of jewelry. It continued to evolve onto more difficult curved surfaces (fig. 23), allowing VC&A jewelers to create voluptuous shapes that place all of the attention on the stones themselves (figs. 24–27). Highly skilled craftsmen and gemstone specialists are needed to ensure not only that all the stones are exactly the right color, but also cut exactly to fit the channels. Emeralds are particularly difficult to use since they are softer and the first cutting methods risk damage when the grooves are created (fig. 28), and since it is extremely challenging to find green emeralds with sufficient saturation and matching of color.

VC&A has continuously refined the Mystery Setting to enable new methods—holding the setting in place on curved surfaces, and "door and screw" mounts on the back placed at intervals for inserting the polished and grooved stones. In 1990, groundbreaking cutting methods enabled VC&A to add diamonds for the first time to the Mystery Setting, and that same year, the hexagonally cut Mystery Setting was added to the repertoire. Nonetheless, the fundamental concept of not revealing any of the setting's support

Fig. 22. "Mystery Setting"
advertisement. Photo reproduction.
Van Cleef & Arpels' Archives

Fig. 23. Mystery-Set Boulle ring. Paris,
France, 1959. Sapphires, yellow gold.
Van Cleef & Arpels' Collection

creates the resulting effect of solid, faceted color, much like a micro-mosaic. In fact, mosaics have been cited as an inspiration for the Mystery Setting. It seems especially likely that the parures and brooches set with micro-mosaic plaques based on antiquity, which became popular in the late eighteenth century and were still evident in 1900 (fig. 29), suggested the concept.

The idea of transformable jewelry has long been a VC&A specialty and the source of many of the firm's most notable technical advancements. A piece that exemplifies all the areas singled out for attention in this exhibition is its Serpent *passe-partout* chain-belt (see Transformations, p. 73). It is a transformable innovation that also reflects the firm's interest in exoticism and fashion and attracted the attention of numerous personalities. Invented in 1939, it functions as a necklace, bracelet, or belt, and has floral clips that double as belt closures and brooches. As a bracelet, it is worn on the upper arm, encircling it like a coiled snake. Among the innumerable famous people to whom it appealed were Paulette Goddard and Doris Duke.

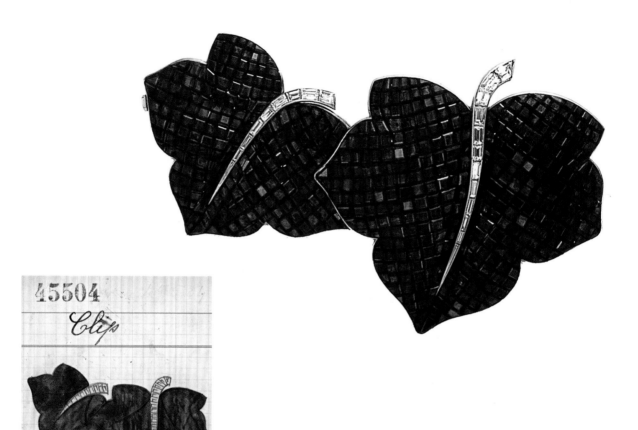

Fig. 25. *Brooch design no. 45504* retail card. Paris, France, 1936. Pigment and ink on card. Van Cleef & Arpels' Archives

Fig. 24. Mystery-Set brooch. Paris, France, 1936. Yellow gold, rubies, diamonds, platinum. Courtesy of Private Collection of Lisa Maria Falcone

Like the Serpent chain, the Zip necklace-bracelet is multifunctional and a splendid technological feat. First conceived around 1938 by VC&A designer René-Sim Lacaze and the Duchess of Windsor, who proposed a piece of jewelry that actually zipped, the Zip necklace with functional zipper mechanism did not appear until 1951 (see Transformations, p. 71). In these intervening years, the zipper became a permanent fixture on clothing, but French jewelry production and design were brought to a near standstill by World War II. What was an avant-garde fashion statement of the late 1930s, when clothing designers intentionally showed off the newly created zipper as visible parts of attire, turned into an avant-garde piece of jewelry some fourteen years later due to its technical prowess.

Fig. 26. Mystery-Set American
Bicentennial brooch. Paris, France,
1976. Rubies, sapphires, diamonds,
platinum. Courtesy of Mrs. Iris Cantor

Fig. 27. Mystery-Set Ribbon bracelet.
Paris, France, 1942. Platinum, rubies,
diamonds. Courtesy of Private
Collection, Chicago

Fig. 28. Mystery-Set Ribbon bracelet
and pair of earrings. New York, NY, ca.
1943. Diamonds, emeralds, platinum.
Courtesy of Mrs. Iris Cantor

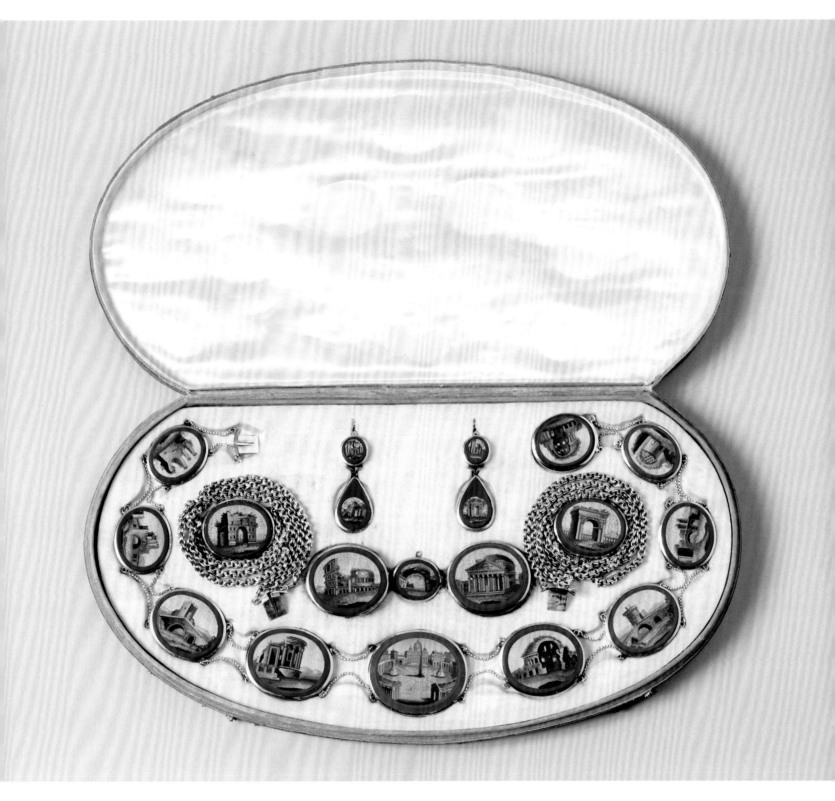

Fig. 29. Suite of micromosaic jewelry. Italy, 1800–25. Gold, glass mosaics. Cooper-Hewitt, National Design Museum, Smithsonian Institution, Gift of Frederick Saal in honor of Dr. and Mrs. Joseph Saal, 1991-160-1/8

Another VC&A innovation was the bracelet known as the "Ludo"—a nickname for Louis Arpels, honored through this design—the first of which appeared in the late 1920s. A bracelet with a buckle closure, it was developed in a number of iterations and its wristband developed in various ways. All of the bracelets incorporated a buckle-like element as the decorative focus, some studded with various gemstones. The earlier versions were usually simple buckles, but with the enthusiasm for bolder and more jeweled designs, the buckles became more dominant (fig. 33). They could incorporate Mystery-Set stones after the jewelers had mastered the art of the curve for this technique, and could even incorporate watches under the curve (fig. 34). One of the most technically challenging bands was the extremely versatile honeycomb band, developed in the late 1930s, formed of flat, interlocking hexagonal elements designed for suppleness. Subsequent elaborations included, in each section, a starburst hole into which a diamond or ruby could be set. Earrings with volutes to match could be acquired to make a set (fig. 35).

With the popularization of the wristwatch during the 1930s, VC&A created a major piece of jewelry in the form of the Cadenas padlock wristwatch (see Peltason, p. 229). The design of this watch, where the face was set at an angle into a curved mount, somewhat resembling a padlock, required two straps to hold it in place, thereby making a double-stranded bracelet. Moreover, the watch face was oriented toward the wearer, thus maintaining her discretion.

World events have been an ongoing source of creativity for VC&A. The challenge of maintaining a luxury business through two World Wars, which led to severe limitations on prized resources such as platinum and gold, led to creative uses of non-precious materials such as wood, glass, leather, enamel, and Styptor, VC&A's name for an alloy that includes aluminum used especially for Minaudières. Many of the creative solutions to difficult times have remained or been revived in new designs over the years, while new materials have been added to the repertoire.

Fig. 30. Zip necklace with extension. Paris, France, 1952. Yellow gold, diamonds. Courtesy of a California Collection

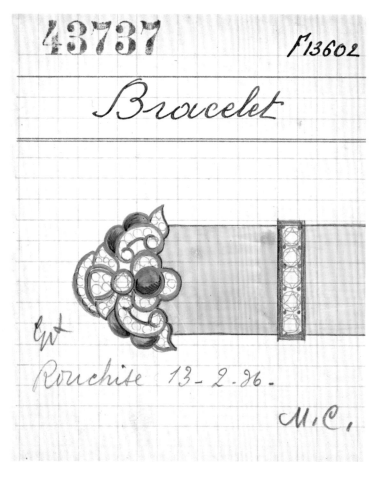

Fig. 32. *Bracelet design no. 43737* retail
card. Paris, France, 1935. Pigment
and ink on card. Van Cleef & Arpels'
Archives

Fig. 31. Ludo bracelet. Paris, France,
1940. Gold, emeralds, diamonds.
Courtesy of Private Collection

Fig. 33. Ludo bracelet. New York, NY,
1940. Platinum, diamonds. Courtesy of
a California Collection

Fig. 34. Ludo bracelet watch. New York, NY, ca. 1940. Yellow gold, aquamarine. Courtesy of Cristina Monet-Palaci Zilkha

Fig. 35. Ludo bracelet and pair of brooches. Paris, France, 1937. Gold, rubies. Courtesy of the Neil Lane Collection

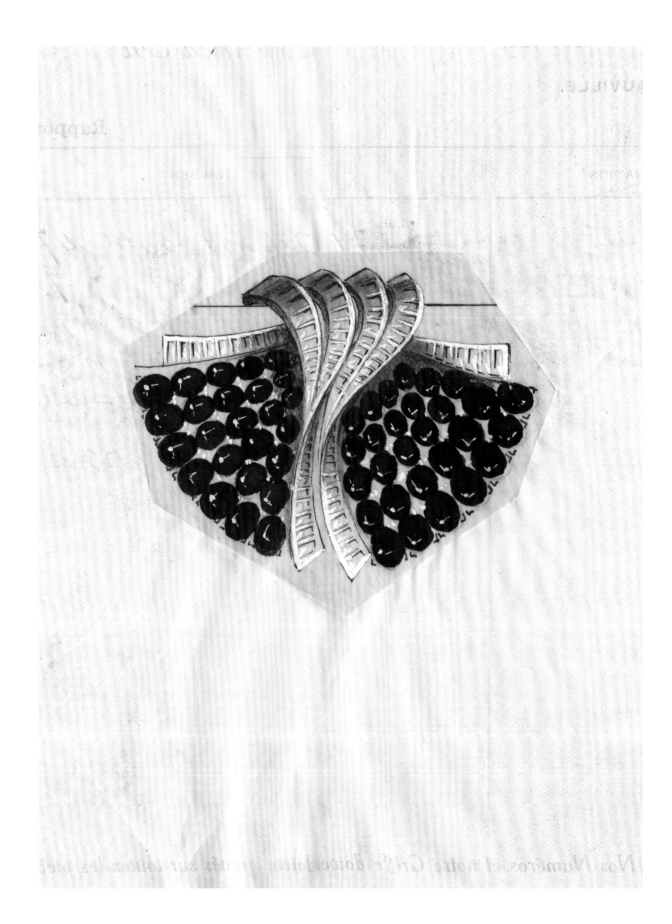

The Arpels arrived in New York for the World's Fair in 1939, once again recognizing their interest in displaying their latest designs to a broader American and worldwide audience. Not only was the World's Fair an important place to show their design innovations, but on the eve of war in Europe, the Arpels stayed in New York and opened a store on Fifth Avenue. This innovation in their business brought new styles to the United States and started VC&A on a distinctly American focus. An effusive period of celebration followed the end of World War II. VC&A featured novel designs including torches, a bird of peace, an open birdcage (during the war it had been closed), and other themes associated with liberation in Paris. Once again, Paris returned as a place to visit and looked to a new life in the arts and fashion, and VC&A could resume a leading role. Thanks to the loyalty and careful accounting of Alfred Langlois and other employees after the Arpels' relocation to New York during the war, the family received the Paris firm back with every penny accounted for. Nonetheless, New York remained the home base for Claude Arpels, and Louis and Jacques continued to commute back and forth to supervise design and production operations.

A steady flow of designs emanated from Van Cleef & Arpels in Paris and in New York in subsequent years. In 1950, to herald the 200th anniversary of the place Vendôme in Paris, VC&A released a line of jewelry inspired by the Enlightenment, referencing an earlier era of French strength, as they hoped to reestablish Paris as a center of twentieth-century enlightenment. One of the objects was a cigarette lighter in the form of the column on the place Vendôme in 1951 (see Transformations, p. 90). In 1958, jewelry with Thai motifs was created for Queen Sirikit of Thailand. VC&A produced new Art Deco–inspired pieces to coincide with a landmark 1966 exhibition on the subject at the Musée des Arts Décoratifs in Paris. A brooch commemorated the American astronauts' walk on the moon in 1969 (see Transformations, p. 101).

While always looking for innovations, VC&A's creative process has in many respects remained the same over the course of many decades. A designer executes a drawing, often a watercolor, to show color (fig. 36). An order sheet and often a separate card (fig. 37) are made up, specifying the number, type, size, and cut of stones to be used, as well as the materials and specifications of the mounts. A unique VC&A order number is added,

Fig. 36. Book spread showing double fan clip 47732. Paris, France, 1937. Gouache on paper. Van Cleef & Arpels' Archives

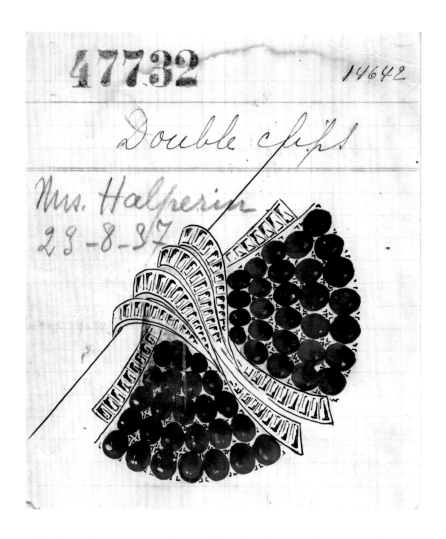

Fig. 37. *Double fan brooch design no. 47732* retail card. Paris, France, 1937. Pigment and ink on card. Van Cleef & Arpels' Archives

which will match the number on the actual piece (fig. 38). In VC&A's extensive archives exist thousands of design concept drawings for objects that were never made, showing the careful selection of design that also is a signature of this process. The art of design continues to this day with design presentation drawings for commissions, designs that live in two dimensions and in the designer's mind before they exist in model forms and later adorn the wearer.

Van Cleef & Arpels' creative solutions, original designs, and technical prowess have contributed to its continued artistic importance for over one hundred years. The firm's designers, master jewelers, cutters, engravers, and other artisans are devoted to solving what are essentially design challenges—which gemstones or techniques best serve a particular design, or how a bangle bracelet with large stones can securely stay on the wrist. The result is an espousal of innovation devoted to the craft of enhancing the beauty of exceptional stones.

Fig. 38. Double Fan brooch. Paris, France, 1937. Platinum, diamonds, rubies. Van Cleef & Arpels' Collection

Volutes Minaudière. Paris, France, 1935.
Yellow gold, black lacquer, diamonds.
Van Cleef & Arpels' Collection

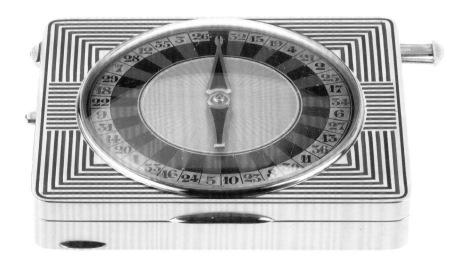

Roulette box. Paris, France, 1926.
Yellow gold, black and red enamel. Van
Cleef & Arpels' Collection

Minaudière. Paris, France, 1934. Yellow gold, styptor, sapphires. Van Cleef & Arpels' Collection

Minaudière. New York, NY, 1944. Gold, styptor, rubies. Courtesy of a California Collection

Brooch-pendant. Paris, France, 1924.
Platinum, diamonds, sapphires, rubies,
emeralds, black enamel. Van Cleef &
Arpels' Collection

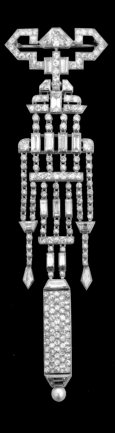

Châtelaine lapel watch. Paris, France,
1927. Diamonds, platinum, pearl.
Courtesy of Neil Lane Collection

Brooch. Paris, France, ca. 1930.
Platinum, natural pearl, diamonds. Van
Cleef & Arpels' Collection

Cornucopia bracelet. Paris, France,
1924. Sapphires, diamonds, platinum.
Courtesy of Private Collection, New
York

Bracelet. Paris, France, 1924. Platinum,
diamonds. Courtesy of Private
Collection

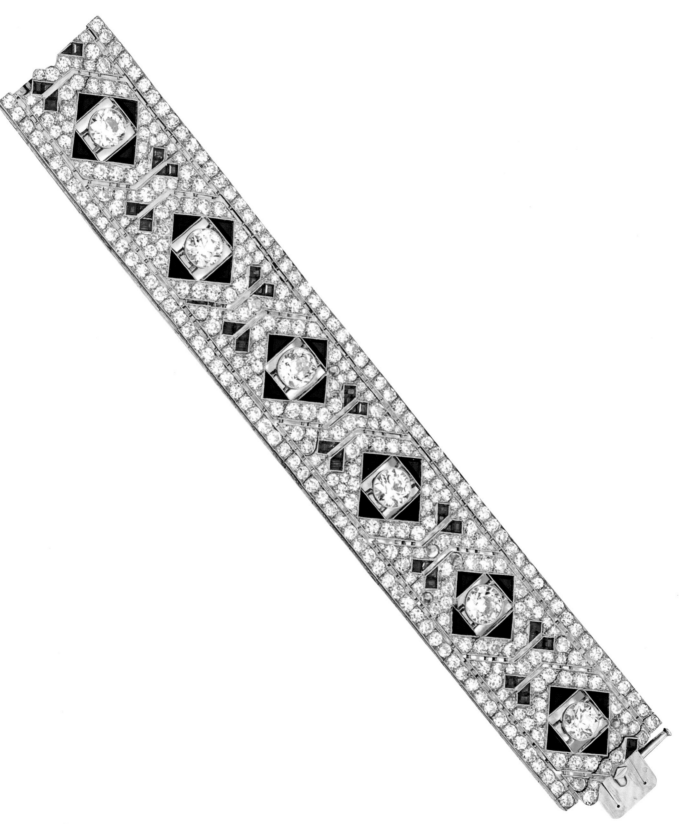

Bracelet. Paris, France, ca. 1930.
Platinum, onyx, sapphires, diamonds.
Courtesy of Private Collection of Lisa
Maria Falcone

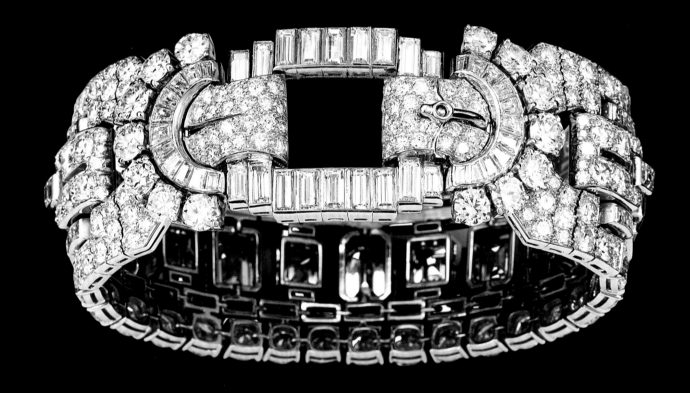

Art Deco bracelet. Paris, France, 1935.
Platinum, diamonds. Van Cleef & Arpels'
Collection

Brooch. Paris, France, 1924. Platinum,
rock crystal, sapphires, diamonds. Van
Cleef & Arpels' Collection

Art Deco bracelet. Paris, France, ca.
1930. Platinum, rock crystal, diamonds.
Courtesy of Paul Fisher

Bracelet. Paris, France, 1935. Rock
crystal, gold. Courtesy of Neil Lane
Collection

Bracelet. Paris, France, 1934. Rock
crystal, gold. Courtesy of Private
Collection, Chicago

Cambodian Roll bracelet. Paris, France, 1938. Moonstones, rubies, diamonds, yellow gold. Courtesy of Private Collection, United States

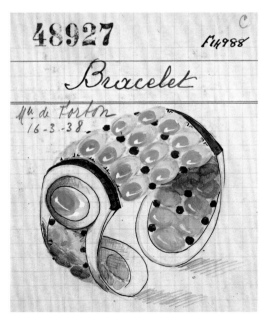

Bracelet design no. 48927 retail card. Paris, France, 1938. Pigment and ink on card. Van Cleef & Arpels' Archives

Earrings. Paris, France, 1935. Diamonds,
sapphires, platinum. Van Cleef & Arpels'
Collection

Bracelet. Paris, France, 1938. Sapphires,
diamonds, platinum. Courtesy of Private
Collection of Lisa Maria Falcone

Bracelet. Paris, France, 1937. Gold,
platinum, sapphires, diamonds. Van
Cleef & Arpels' Collection

Pair of earrings. Paris, France, 1936.
Platinum, diamonds. Courtesy of a
California Collection

Bracelet. New York, NY, 1960. Platinum,
diamonds. Courtesy of Private
Collection

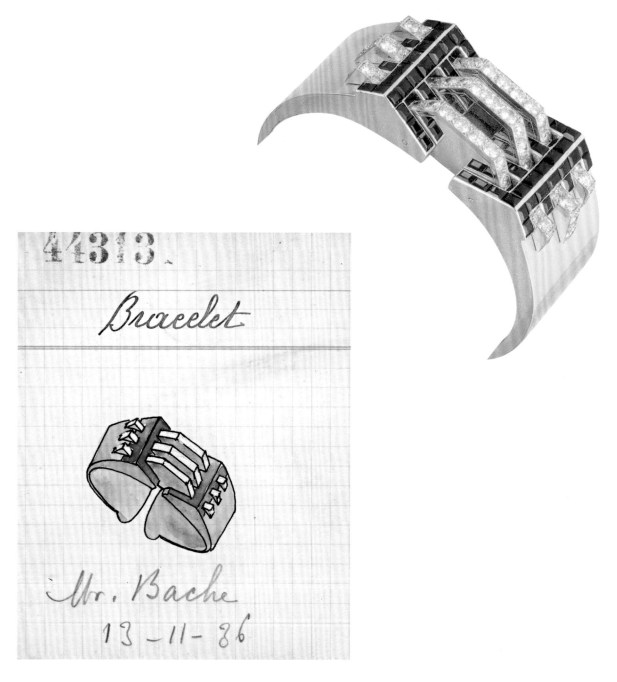

Bracelet design no. 44313 retail card.
Paris, France, 1936. Pigment and ink on
card. Van Cleef & Arpels' Archives

Articulated bracelet. Paris, France,
1936. Red gold, platinum, sapphires,
diamonds. Van Cleef & Arpels'
Collection

Pylones pair of brooches. Paris, France, 1939. Yellow gold, sapphires. Courtesy of a California Collection

Pylones ring. Paris, France, ca. 1939. Yellow gold, sapphires. Courtesy of a California Collection

Choker. Paris, France, 1937. Diamonds,
platinum. Courtesy of The Al Dalaliya
Collection c/o Symbolic & Chase

Bracelet. Paris, France, ca. 1930.
Emeralds, diamonds, platinum, gold.
Courtesy of Private Collection, New
York

Foliage necklace. Paris, France, 1959.
Platinum, gold, rubies, diamonds.
Courtesy of Private Collection, United
States

Tassel pendant pair of earrings. Paris,
France, 1924. Platinum, sapphires,
diamonds. Courtesy of Private
Collection

Mystery-Set Disc pair of earrings. Paris,
France, 1936–37. Rubies, diamonds,
gold, platinum. Courtesy of Private
Collection, Chicago

Peony brooches. Paris, France, ca. 1937.
Gouache on paper. Van Cleef & Arpels'
Archives

Joined Wave brooch. Paris, France,
1943. Yellow gold, sapphires. Courtesy
of Private Collection

Pair of passementerie earrings. Paris,
France, 1948. Rubies, gold. Courtesy of
Jean S. and Frederic A. Sharf

Hexagon Tassels bracelet. Paris, France,
1946. Yellow gold, diamonds. Courtesy
of a California Collection

Brooch. New York, NY, 1950.
Turquoises, rubies, diamonds, yellow
gold. Courtesy of Jean S. and Frederic
A. Sharf

Bracelet. New York, NY, 1945.
Turquoises, rubies, diamonds, yellow
gold. Courtesy of Primavera Gallery,
New York

Tourbillon ring. Paris, France, 1951.
Yellow gold, platinum, diamonds. Van
Cleef & Arpels' Collection

Flexible Bangle Cross-over bracelet.
Paris, France, ca. 1955. Yellow gold,
diamonds. Courtesy of a California
Collection

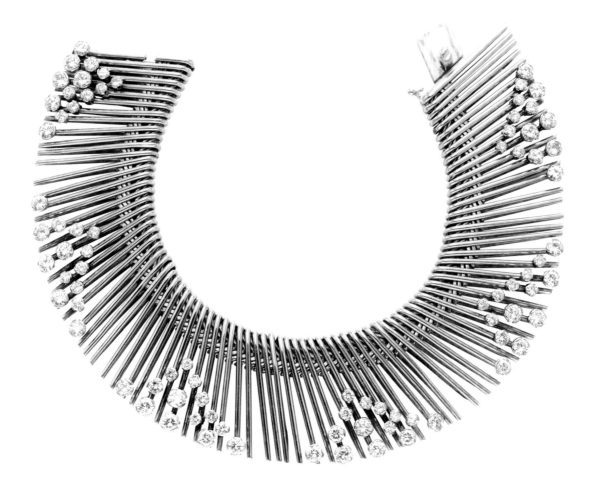

Angel Hair bracelet. Paris, France, 1947.
Yellow gold, diamonds. Courtesy of
Private Collection, Chicago

Natte bracelet. Paris, France, 1967.
Platinum, diamonds. Courtesy of
Anonymous Lender

Pencil holder with perpetual calendar.
Paris, France, 1928. Yellow gold, blue
and white enamel. Van Cleef & Arpels'
Collection

Pocket watch. Paris, France, 1933.
Styptor, yellow gold. Van Cleef & Arpels'
Collection

Brooch/clasp for a bag. Paris, France,
1932. Platinum, chalcedony, diamonds.
Van Cleef & Arpels' Collection

Shantung drawer watch. Paris, France,
1966. Yellow gold, diamonds, enamel.
Van Cleef & Arpels' Collection

Drawer watch. Paris, France, 1966.
Yellow gold, diamonds, enamel. Van
Cleef & Arpels' Collection

Necklace. New York, NY, 1970. Yellow
gold, baroque pearls, diamonds.
Courtesy of Private Collection

Flying Butterfly ring. Paris, France, 2001.
Platinum, diamonds. Courtesy of Van
Cleef & Arpels

By Sarah D. Coffin

TRANSFORMATIONS

Transformation has been a key part of Van Cleef & Arpels' history since its founders converted their heritage of diamond and stone-cutting in the Netherlands and Belgium into one of Paris's top jewelry houses, with an international clientele. Subsequent transformation occurred when the firm opened in New York and produced jewelry to fit an American aesthetic. Transformation also informs VC&A's designs. The idea of a unique object which, through feats of design, craft, and innovative technology, becomes something else entirely is part of VC&A's pedigree.

OBJECTS TRANSFORMED

Transformations can happen through the simple opening of a clasp, or are themselves the product of elements from an earlier piece of jewelry. One necklace with pendant, owned by the Aga Khan and worn by the Begum (Salimah) Aga Khan, has two layers of transformation. First, it comprises eighteenth-century Indian carved emeralds which VC&A composed into a major piece of twentieth-century jewelry, with a reference to historic traditions in a Western context. The suite also changes from a longer necklace to a choker with or without pendant when a section is removed, which itself can be worn as two bracelets (figs. 1, 2).

Models of ancient coins (fig. 3), Chinese snuff bottles and carvings (fig. 4), and other articles from other contexts past and present have been turned into jewelry by VC&A's creative hands. The last was also transformed into a clock through skillful harmonizing of stones in its cylinder base.

The "Zip" necklace was a major VC&A design creation, whose initial triumph lay in the technical feat of its functional zipper action of interlocking gold teeth and in the adjustable size of its opening, all on a necklace/bracelet set with precious stones. Between

Fig. 14a. Walska brooch/pendant. New York, NY, 1971. Yellow gold, sapphires, yellow diamonds (briolette 95 carats), white diamonds. Courtesy of Private Collection

Fig. 1. Aga Kahn choker with pendant. Paris, France, 1971. Yellow gold, carved emeralds, diamonds. Van Cleef & Arpels' Collection

Fig. 2. Aga Khan bracelet (one of a pair, combinable to form a choker). Paris, France, 1971. Gold, carved emeralds, diamonds. Van Cleef & Arpels' Collection

the first concept around 1938 and the actual first execution in 1951, the increased popularity of exposed zippers brought expanded interest in the design's possibilities. It reached its fullest development when the necklace could be opened all the way as well as closed entirely, becoming a bracelet through the removal of a segment from the back of the necklace for a bracelet clasp (figs. 5a–c). Another piece was the *passe-partout* chain necklace, belt, or serpent bracelet, usually studded with floral combinations of precious stones that served to fix the length of the necklace, act as a belt buckle, or as decoration when the chain wrapped around the upper arm (figs. 6a, 6b, 7).

Various necklaces become bracelets and vice versa—featuring sliding tassels or more complicated combinations (figs. 8, 9). The *manchette* bracelets owned by Daisy Fellowes (see Menkes, p. 246) combine to form a necklace. More recent manifestations include a gold, coral, and diamond necklace with pendant that transforms itself into two bracelets (fig. 10). A bracelet can be added into a necklace to lengthen it and pendants attached or detached (figs. 11, 12).

One of the most remarkable such objects is a jeweled bird, carrying a bundle—a 95-carat pear-form yellow diamond—previously owned and worn as a pendant by the opera diva and aspiring socialite Ganna Walska in the 1930s. The diamond appeared at a Sotheby Parke Bernet auction in 1971, and the next year appeared on the cover of the VC&A catalogue in the mouth of the bird, a separate design adapted for this purpose, with a backdrop of the place Vendôme (fig. 13). It was a present commemorating the birth of the owners' son in 1972. The bird, itself a convertible brooch, transforms the role of the yellow diamond, which left its nest in Miss Walska's décolleté to become a prized bundle pendant from the bird's beak, much like the apocryphal stork delivering a baby. The diamond can still be worn as a pendant alone, while the bird, like a phoenix rising from the ashes, can become, through the removal of its wings and tail, a pair of wing earrings and a brooch (figs. 14a, 14b). The diamond still has its own history, but is given new meaning by the bird without a single facet being changed.

The Minaudière, cited as a major VC&A innovation in the previous chapter, turned the eighteenth-century nécessaire into a modern object. Moreover, it goes beyond its appearance as a precious box-form clutch with or without fabric frame and handle, opening to display a treasure trove of useful objects. The rectangular exterior is barely visible when all its parts are pulled out: lipstick, watch, cigarette holder, lighter, comb, mirror, compact and pillbox all emerge (fig. 15; see also Innovation, p. 26).

Fig. 3. Alexander the Great medallion
pendant. New York, NY, 1968. Yellow
gold. Van Cleef & Arpels' Collection

Fig. 4. Table clock–cigarette case made from a Chinese snuff bottle. Paris, France, 1930. Yellow gold, carved turquoise, onyx, lapis lazuli, blue enamel. Van Cleef & Arpels' Collection

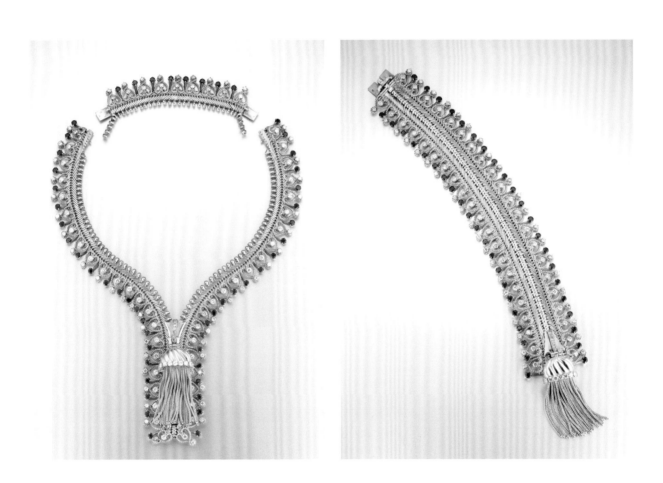

Figs. 5a–c. Zip necklace with extension. Paris, France, ca. 1955. Gold, rubies, diamonds. Courtesy of a California Collection

Figs. 6a, 6b. *Passe-partout* necklace.
Paris, France, 1947. Yellow gold, blue
and yellow sapphires, diamonds, rubies.
Courtesy of a California Collection

Figs. 6a, 6b. *Passe-partout* necklace.
Paris, France, 1947. Yellow gold, blue
and yellow sapphires, diamonds, rubies.
Courtesy of a California Collection

Fig. 7. Special order book, page spread
showing Passe-partout. Paris, France,
1938. Gouache and ink on paper. Van
Cleef & Arpels' Archives

Fig. 8. Tassel and Slide necklace. New York, NY, 1954. Yellow gold, diamonds. Courtesy of Jean S. and Frederic A. Sharf

Fig. 9. Tassel and Slide bracelet. New
York, NY, 1939. Platinum, diamonds.
Courtesy of a California Collection

Fig. 10. *Drapé* necklace with detachable
pendant (separates into bracelets,
part of a set; see Exoticism, p. 179).
Paris, France, 1974. Yellow gold,
coral, diamonds. Van Cleef & Arpels'
Collection

Fig. 11. Necklace, bracelet and pair of earrings. New York, NY, 1974. Onyx, coral, diamonds, yellow gold. Courtesy of Waldmann, Inc.

VC&A has also translated paintings into jewelry. A cigarette box owned by the Maharani of Baroda included on its lid a scene of the Empress Eugénie and the ladies of her court, the luxurious fabrics of their dresses encrusted in gemstones and surrounded by engraving, taken directly from a painting by Franz-Xaver Winterhalter (fig. 16), perhaps subtly comparing the power and style of the Maharani to that of the Empress of France. In another example, a remarkable brooch depicts a dancer—a subject that became a VC&A trademark in the 1940s—who is identified as La Camargo, an eighteenth-century performer who can be seen in exactly the same pose as in Nicolas Lancret's painting of her in the Wallace Collection (figs. 17–19).

The famous column in Paris's place Vendôme was made into its miniature as a cigarette table lighter and given a strike and sold to Hussein Pasha in 1951 after being part of an exhibition on the Enlightenment, transforming the meaning of another era into an object of its day (figs. 20a, 20b, 21). An example of one design object becoming another was the adaptation of a limousine radiator grille as a watch cover or bag clip (figs. 22, 23). The grille could be turned open on a knob to allow a surreptitious glance at the time, especially when used as a lapel brooch. The idea of using a car part for a piece of jewelry is more easily understood when one realizes how few people had cars in the 1920s and 1930s. They were for the rich, and the idea of speed was part of the glamorous world of high fashion and jewelry. A nécessaire featured the speeding lines of a car and train in a 1930 race to Cannes of the Train Bleu and a high-speed roaster (fig. 24). Small clocks or watches were set into decorative boxes of wood or gold or bracelets (figs. 25, 26a, 26b) to facilitate travel and discretion. A Sarpech Hindu brooch (fig. 27) apparently started life as a two-part bracelet (fig. 28) that may have been usable as two brooches or remodeled to create brooches with Hindu-style decoration.

WORLD EVENTS

Transformation is at the very heart of the Van Cleef & Arpels story. Its owners came to New York in 1939, first for the business opportunity of the World's Fair, and then stayed of necessity as war broke out in Europe. With a long list of American clients, they shifted their focus to suit the tastes of their customers and bring them fresh design ideas. VC&A also had to adjust the look of its jewelry to account for available materials. In the United States, platinum was accessible only for military use, so the work had to be done in gold.

Fig. 12. *Vague* (wave) suite: necklace with extension, bracelet, and earrings. Paris, France, 1947. Yellow gold, platinum, diamonds. Courtesy of a California Collection

Fig.13. Catalogue cover with Walska
brooch. Paris, France, 1972. Printed
paper. Van Cleef & Arpels' Archives

Fig. 14b. Walska brooch/pendant,
alternate view. New York, NY, 1971.
Yellow gold, sapphires, yellow
diamonds (briolette 95 carats),
white diamonds. Courtesy of Private
Collection

Fig. 15. Minaudière. New York, NY, 1944.
Gold, styptor, rubies. Courtesy of a
California Collection

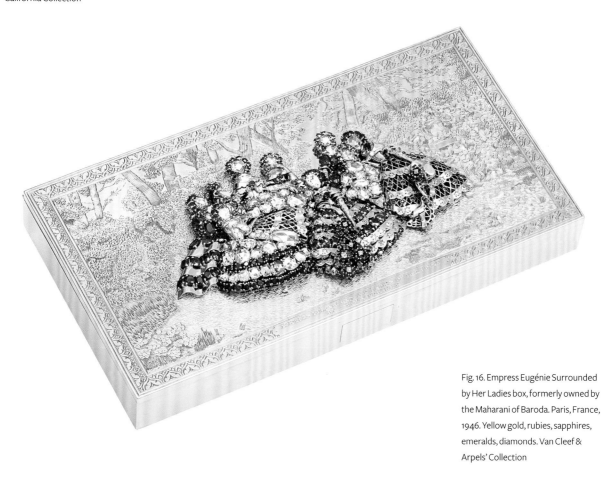

Fig. 16. Empress Eugénie Surrounded
by Her Ladies box, formerly owned by
the Maharani of Baroda. Paris, France,
1946. Yellow gold, rubies, sapphires,
emeralds, diamonds. Van Cleef &
Arpels' Collection

Fig. 17. *Mademoiselle de Camargo Dancing*, 1730. Nicolas Lancret. Oil on canvas. Courtesy of the Trustees of the Wallace Collection, London

Fig. 18. Book page spread showing Camargo ballerina brooch. Gouache and ink on paper. Van Cleef & Arpels' Archives

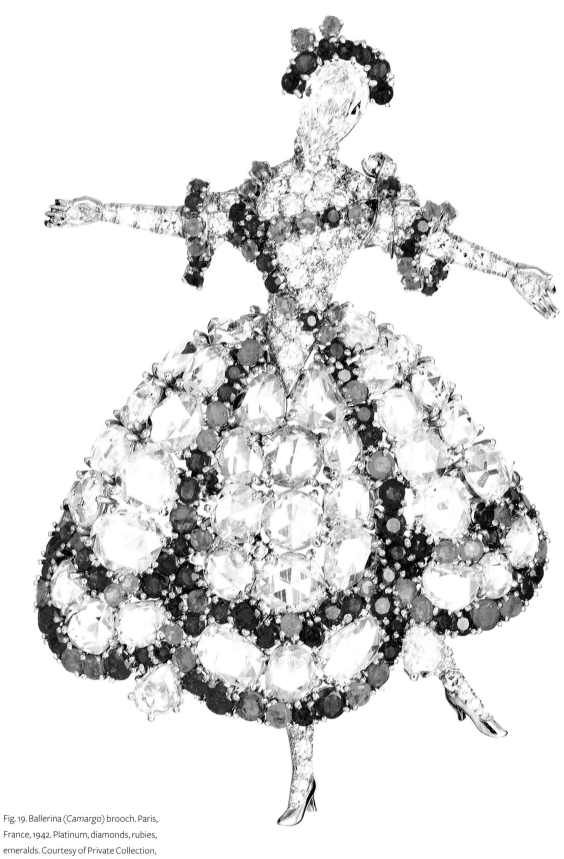

Fig. 19. Ballerina (*Camargo*) brooch. Paris,
France, 1942. Platinum, diamonds, rubies,
emeralds. Courtesy of Private Collection,
United States

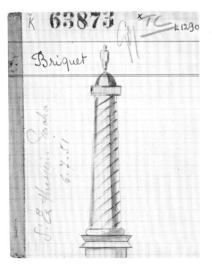

Figs. 21a, 21b. Colonne Vendôme lighter. Paris, France, 1951. Yellow gold. Van Cleef & Arpels' Collection

Fig. 20. *Colonne Vendôme Cigarette Lighter Design no. 63873* retail card. Paris, France, 1951. Pigment and ink on card. Van Cleef & Arpels' Archives

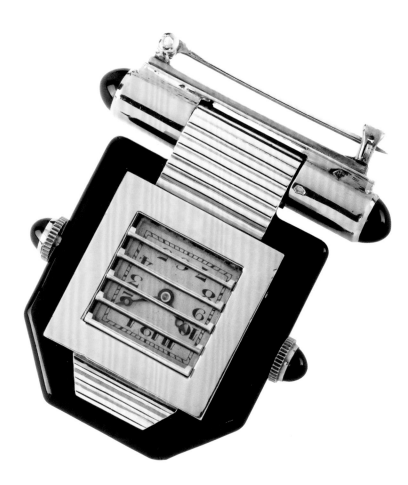

Fig. 22. Radiator lapel/clasp watch. Paris,
France, 1930. Yellow gold, platinum,
onyx. Van Cleef & Arpels' Collection

Fig. 23. Radiator lapel/clasp watch on
bag. Paris, France, 1931. Leather, white
gold, yellow gold, onyx, black lacquer.
Van Cleef & Arpels' Collection

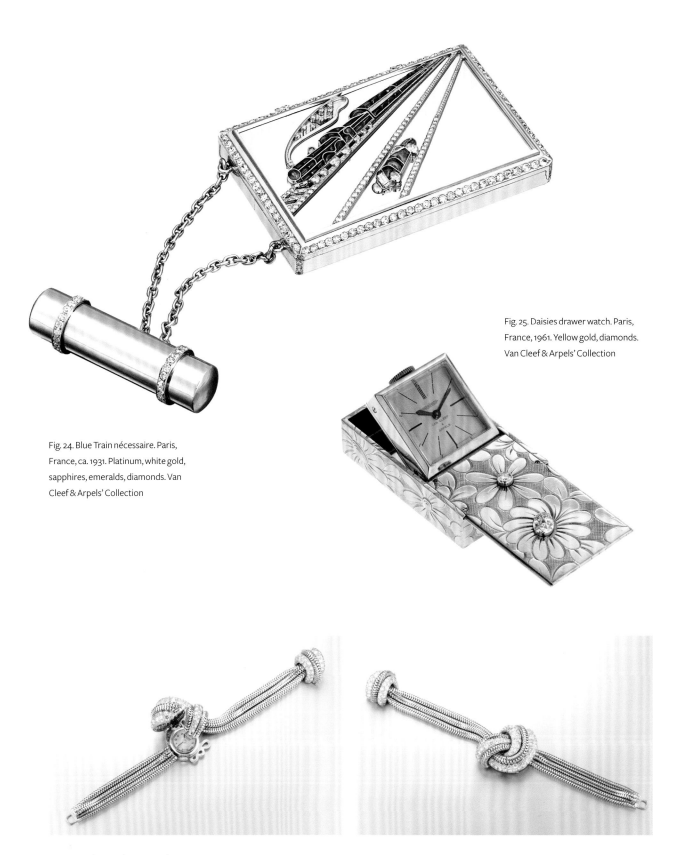

Fig. 24. Blue Train nécessaire. Paris, France, ca. 1931. Platinum, white gold, sapphires, emeralds, diamonds. Van Cleef & Arpels' Collection

Fig. 25. Daisies drawer watch. Paris, France, 1961. Yellow gold, diamonds. Van Cleef & Arpels' Collection

Figs. 26a, 26b. Bracelet. New York, NY, 1954. Yellow gold, diamonds. Courtesy of a California Collection

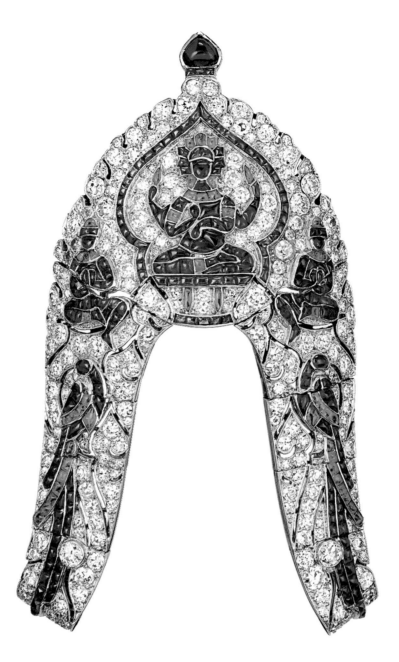

Fig. 28. *Hindu bracelet Design no. 24624* retail card. Paris, France, 1924. Pigment and ink on card. Van Cleef & Arpels' Archives

Fig. 27. Hindu brooch. Paris, France, 1924. Platinum, rubies, diamonds, sapphires, emeralds. Van Cleef & Arpels' Collection

Fig. 29. Swan Lake compact. New York, NY, 1947. Yellow gold, diamonds, sapphires, rubies. Van Cleef & Arpels' Collection

Materials and objects were not available from Paris. The firm there, under stewardship, if it did not have gold already, would have had to ask the client to provide the gold, and the latter was required to turn over 20% of it to the French government if asked. For platinum, the occupied French government regulations generally exacted 135% of any amount used for jewelry, effectively keeping the metal out of jewelry design during the war and for a while afterward.

Dance seems to have had a special connection with VC&A, especially during the era of George Balanchine, who moved to New York in 1933 and co-founded the School of American Ballet. Louis and Claude Arpels had seen the Ballets Russes in Paris in the 1920s, and established a friendship with Balanchine in New York.[1] The inspiration of dance during World War II and in the postwar environment was a grace note in a sober time (fig. 29). VC&A's ballerina, fairy, and cupid (figs. 30, 31) figures, specifically New York market creations, first appeared in the early 1940s. The inspiration for making ballerinas may have been the love of classical ballet that Louis Arpels maintained in New York, where Balanchine was active.

Fig. 30. Spanish Dancer brooch.
New York, NY, 1941. Platinum, rubies,
emeralds, diamonds. Van Cleef &
Arpels' Collection

Fig. 31. Ballerina brooch. New York, NY,
ca. 1940. Platinum, emeralds, diamonds.
Van Cleef & Arpels' Collection

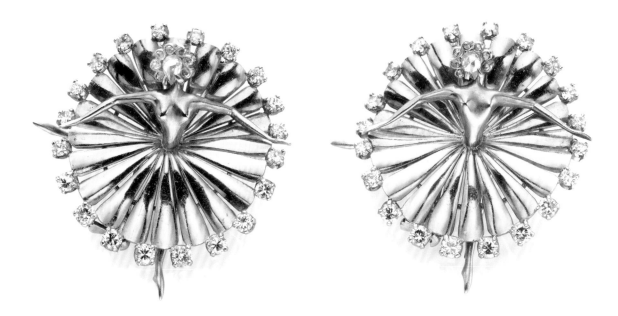

Fig. 32. Ballerina pair of clips. Paris,
France, 1951. Yellow gold, platinum,
diamonds. Courtesy of Private
Collection

Fig. 33. *Ballerina Clip Design no. 64016*
retail card. Paris, France, 1951. Pigment
and ink on card. Van Cleef & Arpels'
Archives

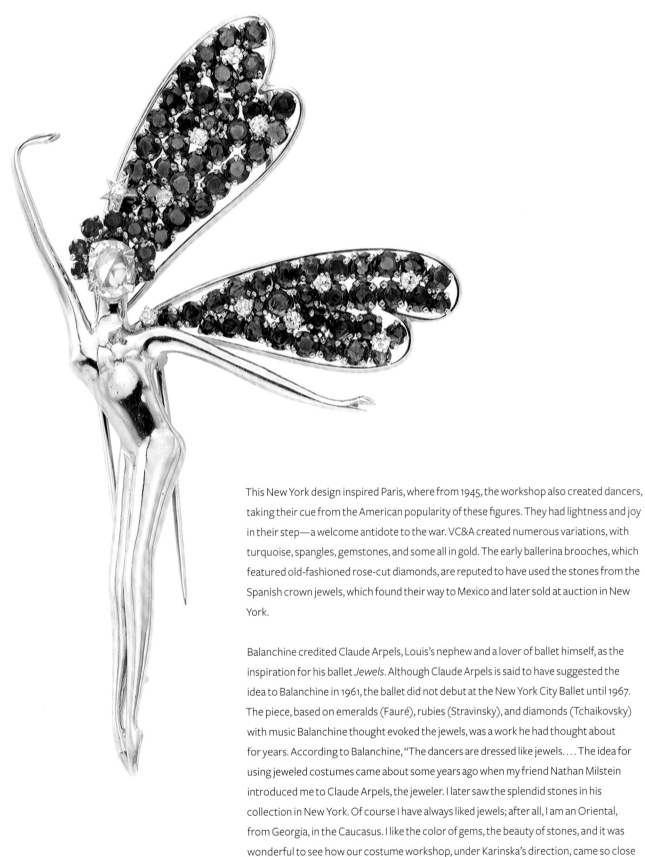

Fig. 34. Tinkerbell brooch. New York,
NY, 1945. Yellow gold, sapphires, rubies,
diamonds. Courtesy of Vartanian &
Sons, Inc.

This New York design inspired Paris, where from 1945, the workshop also created dancers, taking their cue from the American popularity of these figures. They had lightness and joy in their step—a welcome antidote to the war. VC&A created numerous variations, with turquoise, spangles, gemstones, and some all in gold. The early ballerina brooches, which featured old-fashioned rose-cut diamonds, are reputed to have used the stones from the Spanish crown jewels, which found their way to Mexico and later sold at auction in New York.

Balanchine credited Claude Arpels, Louis's nephew and a lover of ballet himself, as the inspiration for his ballet *Jewels*. Although Claude Arpels is said to have suggested the idea to Balanchine in 1961, the ballet did not debut at the New York City Ballet until 1967. The piece, based on emeralds (Fauré), rubies (Stravinsky), and diamonds (Tchaikovsky) with music Balanchine thought evoked the jewels, was a work he had thought about for years. According to Balanchine, "The dancers are dressed like jewels.... The idea for using jeweled costumes came about some years ago when my friend Nathan Milstein introduced me to Claude Arpels, the jeweler. I later saw the splendid stones in his collection in New York. Of course I have always liked jewels; after all, I am an Oriental, from Georgia, in the Caucasus. I like the color of gems, the beauty of stones, and it was wonderful to see how our costume workshop, under Karinska's direction, came so close to the quality of the real stones."[2] Apparently, Claude Arpels suggested the ballerinas wear "jewels" (for this purpose, not real) for a 1976 production with Suzanne Farrells for which Balanchine wrote some new dances.

Fig. 36. Lamp brooch. Paris, France, 1952. Yellow gold, diamonds. Van Cleef & Arpels' Collection

Fig. 35. Cowboy brooch. New York, NY, 1946. Yellow gold, rubies, diamonds. Van Cleef & Arpels' Collection

The dance connection, so important in America, continued VC&A's long tradition of interpreting the arts, and the dance theme is still one of the most cherished among VC&A collectors and enthusiasts. One pair of dancer earrings has an amusing design detail: the bowing dancers, with tutus forming a circle going over their heads, have finished gold backs showing the backside of a dancer, tutu lifted, her underwear and backs of legs exposed (figs. 32, 33). Only the very select could ever see that detail, but the subtle, implied naughtiness makes them even more irresistible.

With a different country came a different set of cultural and aesthetic enthusiasms. The American market was the one for which whimsy became a leitmotif. VC&A's use of lighthearted figures and whimsical animals was particularly popular in the United States. Tinkerbelle appeared in 1945 (fig. 34), cowboys in 1946 (fig. 35). Even a wall sconce became a subject for a brooch (fig. 36). A group of Disney characters, cats with grins, and other creatures followed. These were part of a continuing parade of amusing yet seriously made jewelry that made good jewelry fun. Other objects celebrated significant

Fig. 38. Moon Landing pendant brooch. Paris, France, 1969. Hammered yellow gold, cabochon ruby. Van Cleef & Arpels' Collection

Fig. 37. Liberty Torch brooch. Paris, France, 1944. Yellow gold, platinum, sapphires, rubies, diamonds. Van Cleef & Arpels' Collection

Fig, 39. Globe watch. New York, NY, 1953. Sapphires, diamonds. Courtesy of Neil Lane Collection

Fig. 41. Leaf wristwatch. New York, NY,
1956. Yellow gold, platinum, sapphires,
diamonds. Van Cleef & Arpels'
Collection

Fig. 40. Art Deco ring. Paris, France,
1940. Yellow gold, sapphires, diamonds,
platinum. Van Cleef & Arpels'
Collection

events, most especially the end of World War II, with a torch of liberty brooch (fig. 37).
The 1969 moon landing inspired another (fig. 38). A globe-form watch pendant from the
hand of the Statue of Liberty is a further interpretation (fig. 39).

TRANSFORMATION OF A BUSINESS
When the Arpels left France to exhibit their jewelry at the 1939 New York World's Fair,
they also must have had some extra stock for the business they intended to set up in New
York. A ring made in Paris and sold in New York in 1940 exhibits a technical skill limited
at that time to the skilled jewelers in VC&A's Paris workshop (fig. 40). The Arpels family
soon found skilled workmen in New York to produce new designs.

Jean-Louis Le Henaff, a skilled jeweler in Paris, immigrated to New York with an eight-
year-old son, Jean-Marie, in 1929. When Jean-Marie was twenty-one, looking for more
independence from his father's training, he began working for VC&A under one of its
first New York designers, Maurice Duvalet, a French-born designer who moved to the U.S.
after World War I.[3] Despite the son's connection, the father executed many of the early
VC&A pieces, including some ballerinas along with John Rubel, known as Jean in Paris,
from which he had just emigrated just before World War II. The result was that VC&A
New York secured both Le Henaffs' talents much in the way the firm had done with Alfred
Langlois in Paris, later acquiring the workshops of Le Henaff and Langlois as part of the
firm in both New York and Paris.

Transforming itself for the American market, Van Cleef & Arpels also considered its publicity and promotional style. According to Angela Forenza, a longtime director of advertising and marketing at the company, VC&A New York worked as a family business in which the long-term employees came to feel part of the family. Hired as a junior designer right out of the Pratt Institute in 1943, she became known for her understanding of what would sell in the American market and how to present it. She states that the overriding artistic vision came from the Arpels family, who approved all the designs presented by the in-house designers. They (or the Arpels) had hired Europeans, often those with very elegant family backgrounds, such as twin Bourbon princes and a Russian, Count Kutusov, to help sell social cachet to go with the jewelry. As an American, Forenza saw the importance of local ways of marketing, such as window display—including one she did with a Christmas tree festooned with the company's signature snowflake brooches—as well as advertising placement and graphic design. It was in these areas that she felt the American branch led the French in the postwar firm. By the 1950s, VC&A New York had established its own aesthetic identity, using advertising savvy to focus on objects that would sell well in the United States not because they appealed to would-be Europeans, but by emphasizing a more confident American taste in its high-quality jewelry.

In 1966, VC&A New York started the firm's first watch boutique. Before the boutique, clients looking for wristwatches were often sent to Tiffany's. Forenza saw the problem with this, and when a representative for Piaget showed her some spectacular watches with colored dials, including one tiger-eye, which he hoped VC&A would sell, she went to Claude Arpels to pitch the idea. Beginning in 1966, VC&A teamed with Piaget to sell watches with precise movement and sophisticated detailing.[4] No longer did jewelry hide a watch (fig. 41); the watch was now a stunning accessory, often jeweled and with colored dials, for both men and women. Eventually, this led to VC&A's creation of a watch workshop with designers.

In 2001, Van Cleef & Arpels was acquired by the luxury-goods group Richemont, but that has not revised the policy that both VC&A New York and Paris have of eschewing working with outside designers in favor of designers and artisans hired for their understanding of gemstones and their design potential. This has fostered a remarkable aesthetic consistency, allowing gemstones to guide their design potential, rather than designs that impose themselves on the jewelry. A global market may make the place of design less relevant, but VC&A's recognition of the multiple facets of American style has resulted in this taste becoming part of their global design identity. The transformation of its creations and of the impact of its environment has shaped VC&A's design identity with consistency across continents and eras (fig. 42).

Fig. 42. Scylla necklace with detachable clip. Paris, France, 2008. Diamonds, white gold. Courtesy of a Private Collection

Drops pair of earrings. New York, NY,
ca. 1975. Platinum, diamonds. Courtesy
of a California Collection

Tassel and Slide necklace and pair of
earclips. New York, NY, ca. 1958 and
1952. Yellow gold, platinum, diamonds.
Courtesy of Private Collection

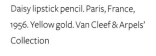

Daisy lipstick pencil. Paris, France, 1956. Yellow gold. Van Cleef & Arpels' Collection

Ropetwist pair of earrings. Paris, France, 1985. Yellow gold, diamonds. Courtesy of Jean S. and Frederic A. Sharf

Place Vendôme cigarette case. Paris, France, 1946. Yellow, pink, and white gold, rubies, sapphires, emeralds, diamonds. Van Cleef & Arpels' Collection

Palm Tree, Birds, Eiffel Tower, Rocking
Horse, Place Vendôme charm bracelet.
Paris, France, 1955–70s. Yellow gold,
diamonds, platinum, rubies, emeralds.
Courtesy of a California Collection

Engagement ring (family heirloom
diamond from a pendant). New York,
NY, 1958. Pink diamond, emeralds,
platinum. Courtesy of Private
Collection

Envelope powder compact. Paris,
France, ca. 1922. Yellow gold, black
enamel. Van Cleef & Arpels' Collection

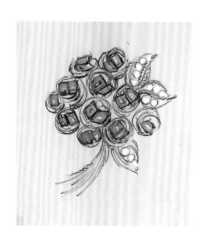

Bouclettes Brooch. Paris, France, 1960.
Gouache and ink on paper. Van Cleef &
Arpels' Archives

Bouclettes brooch. Paris, France, 1960.
Yellow gold, platinum, diamonds, topaz.
Courtesy of Jean S. and Frederic A.
Sharf

Bird and Flower brooch. Paris, France,
1945. Sapphires, diamonds, ruby, yellow
gold. Courtesy of Private Collection

Camellia pair of earrings. New York,
NY, 1956. Diamonds, rubies, platinum.
Formerly owned by the Sadruddin Aga
Khan. Courtesy of Vartanian & Sons,
Inc.

Bracelet. New York, NY, 1969. Yellow
gold, coral, diamonds. Courtesy of The
Al Dalaliya Collection c/o Symbolic &
Chase

By Sarah D. Coffin

NATURE AS INSPIRATION

Nature has inspired jewelry through the ages, and Van Cleef & Arpels is no exception. What differentiated VC&A, right from its inception in 1906, from the lush Art Nouveau interpretations so prevalent at the time were its restraint and its tendency toward stylization and linear pattern as its underlying aesthetic. While a few of the 1910s and early 1920s pieces produced by VC&A emulated nature—for example a bunch of grapes (fig. 1), an orchid (fig. 2), or a seagull (fig. 3) —they still evoked the spirit rather than slavishly copy the object. The choice of diamonds, such as for the orchid, instead of colored stones closest to the natural hues, gives the objects an ethereal presence. Nature also has served as ornament in VC&A objects, such as vanity cases and compacts. In the 1920s, enamel decoration, sometimes of Asian inspiration, incorporated stylized flower heads (figs. 4, 5); another is in the form of an egg that opens, as if cracked, to reveal its contents (fig. 6). Likewise, VC&A roses have no thorns. Flowers, leaves, birds, feathers, butterflies, mushrooms, snails, and snowflakes have all been rendered in signature VC&A fashion (frontispiece and figs. 7–15); as have fauna: lions, cats, hedgehogs, camels, foxes, and poodles (fig. 16 and Peltason, p. 265). These and other more fanciful interpretations, such as Disney creatures, possess a sense of whimsy that has appealed particularly to the American market (figs. 17, 18). So too does a series from the late 1940s and early 1950s of love birds in nests, or "inseparables," most of which take advantage of the rounded surface of the cabochon cut to form the birds' breasts of rubies, sapphires, and occasionally emeralds (figs. 19–21).

Flowers are the most common natural motif for jewelry, and once VC&A perfected a method to incorporate the Mystery Setting securely on box tops, it moved into flowers. The firm's designers often used color-appropriate stones such as rubies to depict naturally red flowers for peonies (see Innovation, p. 10), poppies (figs. 22–24 and Peltason, p. 229), and ranunculi (figs. 25, 26). This last dazzling example was stylized almost beyond

Snowflake brooch. Paris, France, 1948. Yellow gold, diamonds, platinum. Courtesy of Jean S. and Frederic A. Sharf

Fig. 1. Bunch of Grapes brooch. Paris, France, ca. 1915. White gold, silver, seed pearls, diamonds. Van Cleef & Arpels' Collection

Fig. 2. Orchid brooch. Paris, France, 1928. Platinum, diamonds. Van Cleef & Arpels' Collection

Fig. 3. Seagull hat pin. Paris, France,
1926. Platinum, diamonds.
Van Cleef & Arpels' Collection

Fig. 3a. Seagull hat pin (detail)

recognition in the service of a stupendous design. By the 1940s, bouquets and clusters of fruit were appropriate vehicles to show off color combinations of stones to best advantage (figs. 27–29) rather than focus on botanical coloration. Smaller flowers inspired exuberant sprays of decoration (figs. 30–32). Large stones occasionally formed the inspiration for imaginary flowers for which they created petals, as in an aquamarine brooch (see Menkes, p. 205).

While VC&A's renditions of different types of leaves usually have a botanical basis, they remain stylized interpretations of their fundamental shapes. Often, pieces may feature stones whose colors differ from those of the actual plants that inspired them. As leaves were frequently used forms for the Mystery Setting as it spread from boxes to jewelry (figs. 33–35), they may also provide a key to the departure from nature-coordinated colors as being more than a desire for variety. This impulse toward multiple colors for the same leaf may stem partially from the fact that the emerald, the logical stone for most leaves, is an extremely difficult stone to use for the Mystery Setting. Softer than the ruby and sapphire, it is more prone to crack during the required grooving process.

Butterflies—stone-encrusted or wiry, with more insect-like lines and jewels defining their parts—have been a recurring motif throughout the history of the firm (fig. 36). The insect's intricate patterns and shimmering, fleeting effects have been interpreted in a host of materials, from mother-of-pearl to enamel. In fact, some current designs for VC&A's butterfly brooches incorporate Japanese lacquer, applied in Japan using traditional techniques (fig. 37). The snowflake has remained a popular motif since its inception in 1946, as its crystalline structure is not dissimilar to a finely cut diamond. The brooch illustrated here (frontispiece), a giant blow-up in gold and diamonds, captures

Fig. 4. Millefiore compact. Paris, France, 1928. Platinum, red and black enamel, jasper, diamonds. Van Cleef & Arpels' Collection

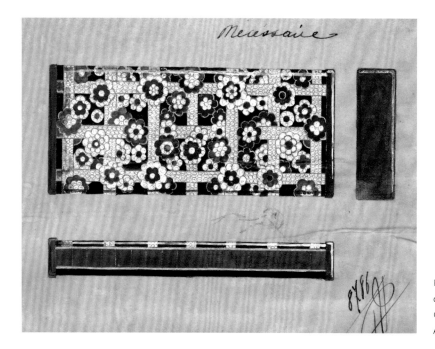

Fig. 5. Book spread showing Millefiore compact 30863. Paris, France, 1927. Gouache and ink on paper. Van Cleef & Arpels' Archives

Fig. 7. Leaves (large and small) pair of clips. New York, NY, 1951. Platinum, sapphires, diamonds. Courtesy of Private Collection, United States

Fig. 6. Egg compact. Paris, France, 1969. Yellow gold. Van Cleef & Arpels' Collection

117

Fig. 8. Bouquet brooch. Paris, France,
1938. Yellow gold, diamonds, blue
enamel. Van Cleef & Arpels' Collection

for posterity the ephemeral sparkle of an individual flake. Like most of VC&A's jewelry designs of the 1940s, either during or just after wartime, the snowflake uses gold and diamonds, as platinum was unavailable or in short supply and severely taxed. Stylization, a primary characteristic of VC&A's designs, so visible in the snowflake, is also visible in designs that feature waves. An Asian-inspired bracelet of the 1920s with naturalistic branch motifs has a strong diamond wave through it (fig. 38). The theme returns in 1970 with sand dollar forms on a bracelet, each with patterns of waves on a granulated ground that suggests waves on the sand (fig. 39). The miniature menagerie that constitutes the animal world of VC&A tended away from faithful portrayals of an animal, such as a 1920s camel, to more fun and fantastical depictions. Along the way, the poodle, a symbol of French chic, retained a realistic appearance, but was given an almost coquettish pose, perhaps to suggest its wearer's persona (fig. 40). The Birds of Paradise series, unveiled in the 1940s, remains popular. It ranges from real to fantasy birds, using the plumage as a source of flamboyant color combinations and swirls (fig. 41). One of VC&A's most successful designs, introduced in 1968, called Alhambra, may suggest Moorish Spain, but it is fundamentally a stylized four-leaf clover, a symbol of luck if found in the grass (see Peltason, p. 230).

Perusing VC&A's renditions of nature, it becomes clear the company views nature as a design opportunity. Rather than simply imitating the natural world, VC&A uses it as a springboard to new creations (figs. 42, 43) that are not merely flowers or an arrangement of stones but a new entity—a piece of jewelry that has its own design.

Fig. 9. Swallow brooch. Paris, France,
1928. Platinum, diamonds. Formerly
owned by Countess Costantini. Courtesy of Private Collection

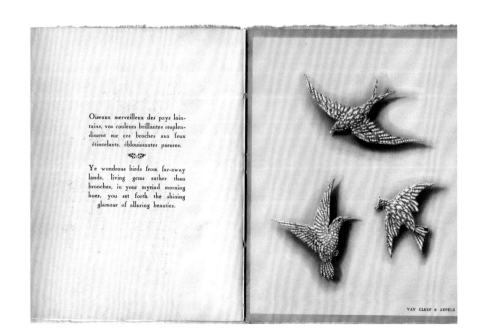

Oiseaux merveilleux des pays loin-
tains, vos couleurs brillantes resplen-
dissent sur ces broches aux feux
étincelants, éblouissantes parures.

Ye wondrous birds from far-away
lands, living gems rather than
brooches, in your myriad morning
hues, you set forth the shining
glamour of alluring beauties.

Fig. 10. Catalogue page
with three bird brooches.
Paris, France, 1923. Printed paper.
Van Cleef & Arpels' Archives

Fig. 11. Sparrow brooch. Paris, France,
1968. Yellow gold, sapphires. Van Cleef
& Arpels' Collection

Fig. 12. Feather brooch. Paris, France,
1928. Platinum, diamonds. Courtesy of
Private Collection

Fig. 13. Butterfly brooch. Paris, France, 1946. Yellow gold, yellow diamonds, sapphires. Van Cleef & Arpels' Collection

Fig. 14. Mushroom brooch. Paris, France, ca. 1968. Yellow gold, rubies, emeralds, sapphires, wood. Van Cleef & Arpels' Collection

Fig. 15. Snail pillbox. Paris, France, 1968. Yellow gold, sapphire. Van Cleef & Arpels' Collection

Fig. 16. Camel brooch. Paris, France, 1926. Platinum, rubies, diamonds. Courtesy of Neil Lane Collection

Fig. 17. Duck brooch. New York, NY, 1965. Baroque pearl, rubies, diamonds, yellow gold. Courtesy of Private Collection

Fig. 18. Scarecrow pin. Paris, France, ca. 1968. Chrysoprase, sapphire, rubies, diamonds, yellow gold. Courtesy of Private Collection

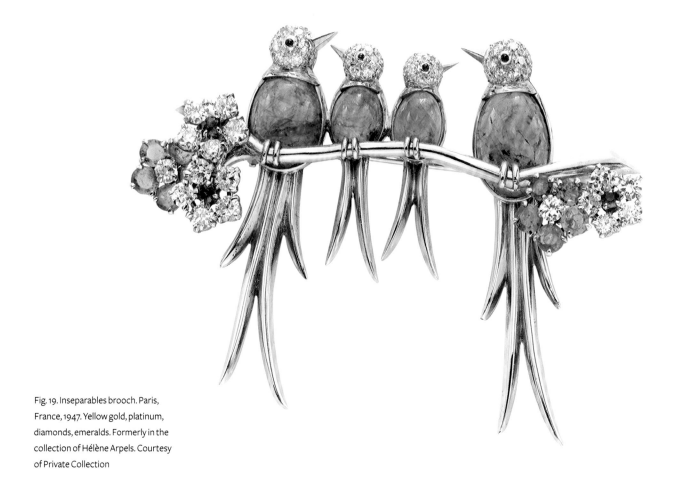

Fig. 19. Inseparables brooch. Paris,
France, 1947. Yellow gold, platinum,
diamonds, emeralds. Formerly in the
collection of Hélène Arpels. Courtesy
of Private Collection

Fig. 20. Inseparables brooch. New
York, NY, 1957. Yellow gold, white gold,
rubies, emeralds, diamonds. Courtesy
of Private Collection

Fig. 21. Inseparables brooch. Paris,
France, 1957. Rubies, diamonds, yellow
gold. Courtesy of Vartanian & Sons, Inc.

Fig. 23. *Flower Brooches*. Paris, France, ca. 1985. Gouache on paper. Van Cleef & Arpels' Archives

Fig. 24. *Flowers*. Paris, France, ca. 1985. Graphite on tracing paper. Van Cleef & Arpels' Archives

Fig. 22. Mystery-Set Flower brooch. Paris, France, 1986. Diamonds, rubies, platinum. Courtesy of Jean S. and Frederic A. Sharf

Fig. 25. Mystery-Set Bouquet brooch.
Paris, France, ca. 1937. Platinum, rubies,
diamonds. Courtesy of a California
Collection

Fig. 26. Mystery-Set Disc earrings.
Paris, France, 1943. Platinum, rubies,
diamonds. Courtesy of a California
Collection

Fig. 27. Hawaii choker. Paris, France, ca.
1939. Gold, sapphires, rubies. Courtesy
of a California Collection

Fig. 28. Fruit Salad bracelet. Paris,
France, 1929. Platinum, emeralds, sap-
phires, rubies, diamonds. Courtesy of a
California Collection

Fig. 29. Bouquet brooch. Paris, France,
1938. Yellow gold, topazes, sapphires.
Van Cleef & Arpels' Collection

Fig. 30. Hawaii brooch. New York, NY,
1946. Gold, rubies, diamonds, sapphires.
Courtesy of Private Collection, Chicago

Fig. 31. Bouquet brooch. Paris, France,
1938. Yellow gold, moonstones, rubies,
diamonds. Courtesy of Private Collection

Fig. 32. Bouquet brooch. Paris, France,
1939. Gold, rubies, sapphires. Courtesy
of Private Collection

Fig. 33. Chestnut Leaf brooch. Paris, France, 1952. Sapphires, diamonds, platinum. Van Cleef & Arpels' Collection

Fig. 35. Three Leaves brooch. Paris, France, 1966. Rubies, diamonds, platinum. Courtesy of Private Collection, New York

Fig. 34. Sycamore Leaf brooch. Paris, France, 1951. Emeralds, diamonds, platinum. Van Cleef & Arpels' Collection

Fig. 37. Kikumakie Butterfly brooch. Paris, France, and Japan (lacquer), 2004. Yellow gold, wood, lacquer, diamonds. Van Cleef & Arpels' Collection

Fig. 36. Butterfly brooch. New York, NY, 1942. Yellow gold, turquoises, rubies, diamonds. Courtesy of Susan Gale

Fig. 40. Poodle brooch. New York, NY, 1953. Gold, diamonds, rubies. Courtesy of a California Collection

Fig. 41. Scarlet Macaw brooch. Paris, France, 1995. Coral, onyx, rubies, sapphires, yellow sapphires, yellow gold. Courtesy of Jean S. and Frederic A. Sharf

133

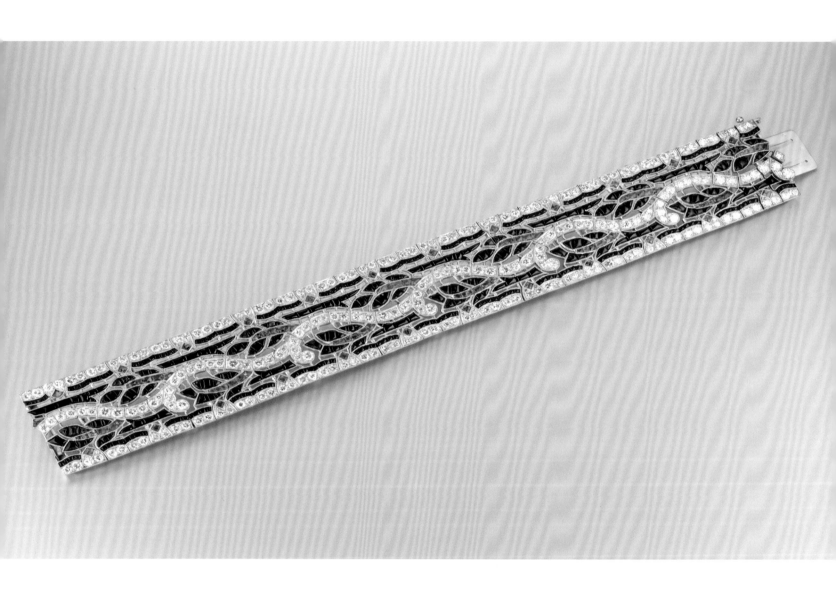

Fig. 38. Bracelet. Paris, France, ca. 1930.
Rubies, emeralds, sapphires, diamonds,
onyx, platinum. Courtesy of a California
Collection

Fig. 39. Mikado and Vagues bracelets.
Paris, France, 1970. Yellow gold. Courtesy of a California Collection

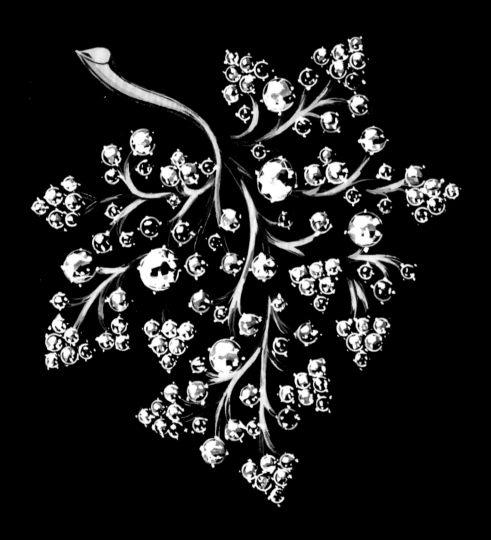

Fig. 42. *Fern brooch*. Paris, France, ca. 1959. Gouache on paper. Van Cleef & Arpels' Archives

Fig. 43. Fern brooch. Paris, France, 1959.
Platinum, diamonds, gold. Van Cleef &
Arpels' Collection

Flower Lace bracelet. Paris, France,
1946. Yellow gold, rubies, diamonds.
Van Cleef & Arpels' Collection

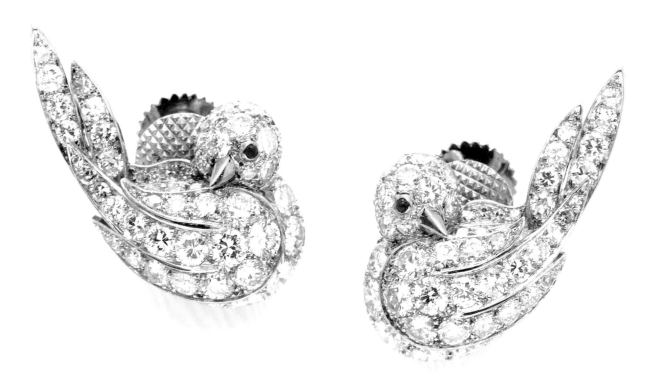

Inseparables earrings. Paris, France, 1956. Platinum, rubies, diamonds. Van Cleef & Arpels' Collection

Inseparables ring. Paris, France, 1961. Yellow gold, rubies, diamonds, platinum. Van Cleef & Arpels' Collection

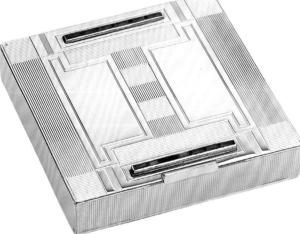

Landscape compact. Paris, France,
1930. Osmoir, yellow gold, rubies, green
and red enamel. Van Cleef & Arpels'
Collection

Clover Bouquet brooch. Paris, France, 1950. Platinum, diamonds. Van Cleef & Arpels' Collection

Flower Head pair of earrings. Paris,
France, 1954. Sapphires, diamonds,
platinum, gold. Courtesy of Private
Collection, Chicago

Two Flowers pair of earrings. New York,
NY, 1955. Gold, platinum, diamonds,
rubies. Van Cleef & Arpels' Collection

Flower Basket brooch. Paris, France,
1927. Diamonds, rubies, emeralds, platinum. Van Cleef & Arpels' Collection

Oak Leaves bracelet watch. Paris,
France, 1951. Yellow gold, rubies, sap-
phires, diamonds. Formerly owned by
King Baudoin of Belgium. Van Cleef &
Arpels' Collection

Flower wristwatch. New York, NY, 1945.
Yellow gold, diamonds, rubies. Van
Cleef & Arpels' Collection

Buttercup brooch design no. 54576
retail card. Paris, France, 1944. Pigment
and ink on card. Van Cleef & Arpels'
Archives

Buttercup brooch. Paris, France, 1944.
Yellow gold, sapphires. Courtesy of
Private Collection, Chicago

Buttercup pair of earrings. Paris,
France, 1944. Gold, diamonds. Courtesy
of Private Collection, Chicago

Bouquet brooch design no. 56639 retail card. Paris, France, 1946. Pigment and ink on card. Van Cleef & Arpels' Archives

Bouquet brooch. Paris, France, 1946. Yellow gold, demantoid garnets. Courtesy of Private Collection

Flowers pair of earrings. New York, NY, 1961. Platinum, diamonds, rubies, yellow gold. Courtesy of Private Collection, Chicago

Flower brooches drawings. Paris, France, late 1930s–late 1950s. Gouache on paper. Van Cleef & Arpels' Archives

Vine leaf. Paris, France, ca. 1937. Gouache on paper. Van Cleef & Arpels' Archives

Leaf brooch design no. 64303 retail card. Paris, France, 1952. Pigment and ink on card. Van Cleef & Arpels' Archives

Snowflake. Paris, France, ca. 1948.
Gouache on paper. Van Cleef & Arpels'
Archives

Bouquet brooch design no. 50899
retail card. Paris, France, 1939. Pigment
and ink on card. Van Cleef & Arpels'
Archives

By Sarah D. Coffin

EXOTICISM

While Van Cleef & Arpels was not alone among the top jewelry firms in seeking out exotic motifs in the 1920s, its global clientele has made exoticism a continued feature of its design aesthetic. An incredibly diverse array of sources of inspiration—from research done by the Arpels family on its travels to the commissions of potentates across the globe—has led to the creation of some of its most distinctive motifs.

Howard Carter and Lord Carnavon's discovery of King Tutankhamun's tomb in 1922 almost immediately had a dynamic effect on the decorative arts and jewelry. Thanks to Napoleon's campaigns in Egypt and his interest in portraying himself as the equal of ancient civilizations, the Egyptian revival's forms and motifs had flourished in early nineteenth-century France more than anywhere else in Europe. King Tut's tomb decorations became instant fodder for French-based designers. VC&A worked the motifs into bracelets (figs. 1, 2), brooches, and pendants with designs rendered with the precision of fine micromosaics or portrait miniatures; even handbags were not immune (fig. 3). VC&A's Egyptian revival work represented some of the best and most meticulous French work produced in the 1920s. Created around 1950, this box of a peacock spreading its wings may have also had its roots in the Egyptian archeological find (fig. 4), although the Persians' love of the peacock motif may have been in play by this date. In fact, the revival was considered almost French, as is evident in an article on French jewelry from the *French Exposition of Arts, Commerce, and Industry* at the Grand Central Palace in New York in 1924, at which VC&A exhibited. A masterpiece of French marketing for Americans before the 1925 Art Deco show in Paris, the exhibition and its publications were aimed to whet the appetite for the French understanding of the exotic as well as for French jewelry. The article, entitled "Jewelry and the Orient," extolled Egyptian jewelry of the Twelfth Dynasty (1991–1783 BC), and noted that "Parisian designers were quick to react to this revival of interest in things Egyptian, the results containing the obvious

Cambodian brooch. Paris, France, 1938. Yellow gold, rubies. Formerly owned by Andy Warhol. Courtesy of Primavera Gallery, New York

149

Fig. 1. Egyptian bracelet (closed and
open). Paris, France, ca. 1924. Emeralds,
rubies, sapphires, diamonds, platinum.
Courtesy of Primavera Gallery, New
York

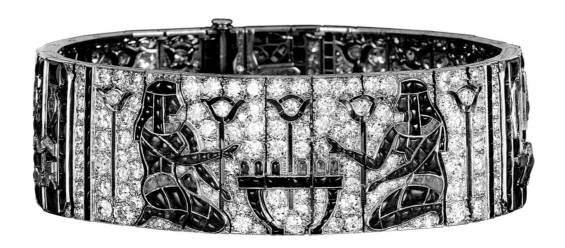

Fig. 2. Egyptian bracelet. Paris, France, 1924. Platinum, sapphires, rubies, emeralds, diamonds. Van Cleef & Arpels' Collection

Fig. 4. Peacock box. Paris, France, ca. 1950. Yellow gold, green and blue enamel, lapis lazuli. Van Cleef & Arpels' Collection

elements of that art with none of the dignified beauty of its best period," although they did commend and illustrate some of these pieces in the exhibition. The article went on to claim that British and American jewelry was not influenced by the various "Oriental" influences, but that in the pieces of French jewelry "the more closely the inspiration springs from the original and follows it the handsomer are the resultant design and workmanship." Just when the authors appear to be condoning slavish copying, they continued, "But in none of these excursions into Oriental designs are the French jewelers as happy as in those forms which are born of the true art genius of their own country.... For the French have a tradition of their own, not alone in the fine arts, but in the crafts as well, from which they can draw rich treasures and to which they can add, with each succeeding generation, new glories."[1] The Egyptian pieces seem to present-day eyes a felicitous mixture of Egyptian sources, VC&A's interpretive designs for gems, and the top-level execution that spoke to their Paris makers.

Illustrative of the exotic styles influenced by a potentate is the Maharani of Baroda's pendant necklace (see Peltason, p. 263), based on Indian necklaces that have existed for many centuries but transformed into a necklace that looks at home in Europe. In an ironic twist, the Maharani of Baroda wanted a necklace more suited to Western tastes, at the same time that the enthusiasm for the exotic led Westerners to look to these interpretations. As a result, this suite, like others produced for Asian grandees influenced many necklace combinations in exotic taste throughout the history of the firm (figs. 5a, 5b; also see Transformations, p. 85).

Fig. 3. Egyptian Odalisque evening bag. Paris, France, 1927. Yellow gold, enamel, silk, rubies, diamonds. Van Cleef & Arpels' Collection

Figs. 5a, 5b. Necklace and pair of
earrings. New York, NY, 1977. Pink
tourmaline, amethyst, diamonds, gold.
Van Cleef & Arpels' Collection

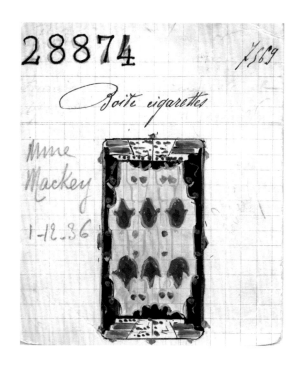

Fig. 6. *Cigarette Case design no. 28874* retail card. Paris, France, 1927. Pigment and ink on card. Van Cleef & Arpels' Archives

Middle Eastern and especially Persian motifs appeared in the 1910s, and were employed by VC&A at various times before the 1931 *Exposition Coloniale Internationale* in Paris. A VC&A design produced by Strauss, Allard, Meyer, with a plaque by the Aronsberg firm, ordered in January 1926 and delivered in 1927 (figs. 6, 7), replicated the idea of a Persian carpet in enamel.[2]

The Ballets Russes provided a significant "exotic" influence on the arts in France. While not directly of influence on Van Cleef & Arpels' jewelry, their use of traditional Slavic motifs and colors, along with elements from the more remote reaches of the Russian Empire, merged the fine and decorative arts with vibrancy. As the Ballets Russes became a sensation in Paris and Monte Carlo, their popularity led to greater demand for color by many of VC&A's clients. Both before and after the Russian Revolution, the corps de ballet and surrounding artists brought with them bright colors and talents, which were often adapted for new artistic endeavors. Well before the revolution, the primary color associated with Russia was red. The archaic meaning of *Krasny*—meaning red—is beautiful. The historical desirability of rubies, the Russian enthusiasm for red, and the associations of red with passion and strength may well have combined to move rubies back into the forefront of haute jewelry design in the "roaring" 1920s.

Chinese culture and design also revere red. The 1920s and 1930s were a period of resurgent interest in China and, to a lesser extent, Japan. Wares inspired by Japan had enjoyed great popularity at the 1878 Paris *Exposition Universelle* but languished in the 1910s. Wealthy travelers visited China in larger numbers starting in the 1890s, and world's fairs prominently displayed Asian wares. Interest in the Far East was rekindled during the 1920s and 1930s, which significantly influenced the choice of color, motifs, and

Fig. 7. Kashmir cigarette case. Paris, France, 1927. Mother-of-pearl, black and green enamel, emeralds, sapphires, amethyst, diamonds, gold, platinum. Van Cleef & Arpels' Collection

157

Fig. 8. *Japanese Pendant Sautoir Design
no. 23731* retail card. Paris, France, 1924.
Pigment and ink on card. Van Cleef &
Arpels' Archives

materials in the decorative arts and jewelry. However, whereas works in the Japonism
style popular at the 1878 World's Fair referenced woodcuts and other graphics in objects
with linear metalwork engraving, a VC&A pendant plaque (fig. 8) of 1924 featured a
pierced composition, almost a painting, with both the Japanese landscape palette
and composition in high-voltage colors of precious stones. A gold-and-black enamel
nécessaire with daisies looks like a Japanese silk bag (fig. 9).

The works in lacquer and enamel of French designer Jean Dunand, represented in
several categories at the famed 1925 Paris *Exposition Internationale des Arts Décoratifs
et Industriels Modernes,* were often in the iron red and black palette inspired by Asian
examples (fig. 10). VC&A responded to the same inspiration with a mixture of Chinoiserie-
decorated objects in enamel, such as a nécessaire (figs. 11, 12), and the use of coral, onyx,
and enamel to create the red and black effects, starting before 1925. The colors of a pair

Fig. 9. Daisy evening bag. Paris, France,
1950. Black lacquer, yellow gold, silver.
Courtesy of a California Collection

of coral and black earrings and bracelet from 1922 and 1923 reflect the significant interest
in Chinese decoration as a source, even though the styles of the objects is more Western

Fig. 12. *Chinese Dragon Nécessaire*
Design no. 22510 retail card. Paris,
France, 1923. Pigment and ink on card.
Van Cleef & Arpels' Archives

Fig. 10. Vase. Designed and made by
Jean Dunand (Swiss, 1877–1942).
France, ca. 1925. Brass, lacquer, nickel.
Cooper-Hewitt, National Design
Museum, Smithsonian Institution, Gift
of Linda Lichtenberg Kaplan, 2004-21-1

Fig. 11. Chinese Dragon nécessaire. Paris, France, 1923. Yellow gold, black and red enamel, jade, diamonds. Van Cleef & Arpels' Collection

Fig. 13. Pair of pendant earrings.
Paris, France, 1923. Platinum, coral,
onyx, diamonds. Courtesy of Private
Collection

Fig. 14. Bracelet. Paris, France, 1923.
Gold, osmior, coral, black enamel,
diamonds. Courtesy of Private
Collection

than in Chinese tradition (figs. 13, 14). Even a pocket watch of 1927 was decorated with a Chinese magician (fig. 15). Japan also added its imprint on VC&A's repertoire.

Coral, onyx, jade, and turquoise, sometimes sculpted, along with engraved stones and natural pearls, much associated with jewelry from other cultures dating back to antiquity, were worked into objects in the Western taste and in combinations of foreign and Western craftsmanship. Likewise, the black and gilt with red enamel châtelaine watch incorporates the style of Chinese lacquer decoration into an object that suited Western fashion tastes—a watch that could hang face-in and decorate a dress as a pendant brooch (fig. 16) was not an Asian conceit. Also Western in its function is a table clock ordered up by the Duchess of Windsor in 1930, which, when closed, looks like a miniature Chinese lacquer cabinet and has a jade dial. The allure of China extended to the American market. A vanity case in blue enamel with a carved jade plaque and diamond clasp opens to reveal a lipstick holder, two compartments, and a mirror, and is engraved "Mrs. R.H. Morse, Chicago" (fig. 17). Another mixed-culture concept was the use of an actual eighteenth-century Chinese perfume bottle set on a VC&A stand with revolving clock (see Transformations, p. 75).

Singer Josephine Baker's appeal lay not only in the supposed "exoticism" of her skin color but also in her new jazz singing style from New Orleans, contributing to the allure of the Western hemisphere. The New World provided more clients than inspiration for jewelry design, but the 1920s witnessed a budding interest in Mayan motifs and pyramids popularized by archeological exploits covered in the world's newspapers. Pyramids, with their stark geometries, are key forms to both Egyptian and Mayan cultures, and readily appealed to the anti–Art Nouveau movement. The pair of earrings illustrated here could have referred to either culture, but is also an avant-garde Art Deco design (fig. 18).

Although VC&A did not exhibit in the first *Exposition Coloniale*, held in Marseille in 1922, they did exhibit in the Paris exhibition in 1931. An idealized portrait of countries once or still part of the colonial empires, the exhibition showed native handicrafts from places such as the Côte d'Ivoire and French objects ostensibly inspired by these cultures or using their raw materials. André Maurois's account from the exhibition, entitled *Sur le vif* (*Drawn from Life*),[3] described some of the architecture and crafts with crayon sketches,

Fig. 15. Chinese Magician pocket watch.
Paris, France, 1927. Yellow gold, enamel,
osmior. Van Cleef & Arpels' Collection

Fig. 16. Châtelaine watch. Paris, France,
1924. Yellow gold, platinum, red and
black enamel, diamonds, pearl. Van
Cleef & Arpels' Collection

Fig. 17. Vanity case. Paris, France, 1925.
Platinum, sculpted jade, enamels,
diamonds. Courtesy of Richters of
Palm Beach

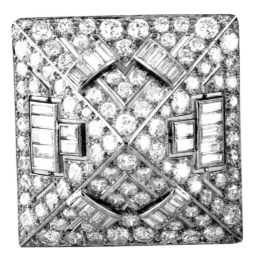

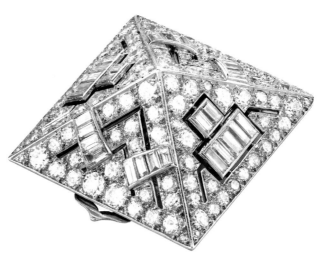

Fig. 18. Pyramid pair of lapel clips. Paris, France, 1920. Gold, platinum, diamonds. Van Cleef & Arpels' Collection

including "charming" minarets. He exhibited greater interest in the contributions of the cosmopolitan cultures of Persia, India, and the Far East, showing this exhibition to be more about looking for new sources and materials to energize the buying public at a time of economic woe than about the cultures of these sources. For this exhibition, a complete suite of jewelry formed of Chinese farmers' hats turned the broad cones into abstract gold designs (figs. 19, 20). The use of materials such as highly grained hardwoods and ivory from Africa and Asia lent a more exotic tone to jewelry and objects produced at this time without precious stones. The idea to create a watch or a small travel clock in wood was a novelty instead of the necessity it might have seemed during World War I.

VC&A also drew on the beauty of French-dominated countries in far-flung places. Cambodia was the source for a bracelet with rotating end to open for fitting on the wrist (fig. 21). An Arpels trip to Morocco in the 1930s is said to have inspired the "Couscous" bands—so named because the beads of gold resemble the dish. The commissioning by Queen Sirikit of Thailand in 1958 for jewelry in the Thai taste acknowledged the importance of VC&A jewelry for a monarch, but also resulted in some Thai-inspired jewelry for marketing (figs. 22–24). While some of the representations of figures from exotic cultures from the 1930s through the 1950s can seem caricatural or quaint to modern taste, most are endowed with humor or whimsy that make them fun if not profound designs. It is this sense of fun that is part of the overall design to appeal to a variety of tastes and ages (fig. 25). Another design first introduced in 1968 to attract

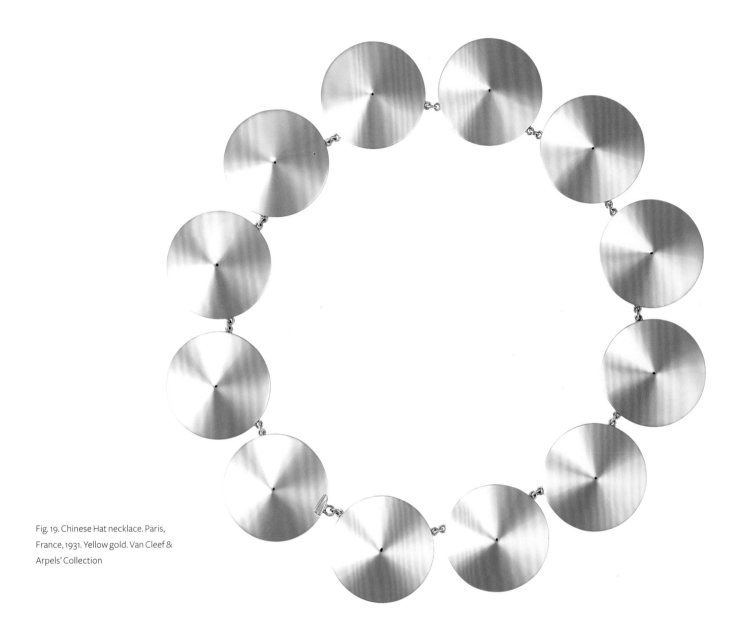

Fig. 19. Chinese Hat necklace. Paris, France, 1931. Yellow gold. Van Cleef & Arpels' Collection

Fig. 20. Chinese Hat ring. Paris, France, 1931. Yellow gold. Van Cleef & Arpels' Collection

Fig. 21. Cambodian bracelet. Paris,
France, 1938. Platinum, diamonds. Van
Cleef & Arpels' Collection

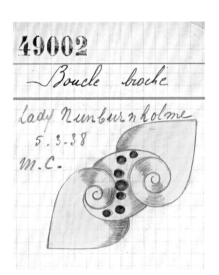

Fig. 22. *Cambodian Brooch Design no. 49002* retail card (See Exoticism frontispiece, p. 148). Paris, France, 1938. Pigment and ink on card. Van Cleef & Arpels' Archives

younger buyers, the clover necklace in gold or gold and enamel, named Alhambra, has a quatrefoil motif between chains that not only looks like a four-leaf clover but also recalls the shapes on the Moorish-inspired tiles and cut-out stone decoration of the Alhambra and other Moorish architecture in southern Spain.

In the 1970s, a blockbuster exhibition, *The Treasures of Tutankhamun*, revitalized enthusiasm for Egyptian motifs (fig. 26). This exhibition started a seven-year tour in London in 1972 and went to France and the United States, where its final stop was the Metropolitan Museum of Art in New York, drawing huge crowds until it closed in 1979. Another larger exhibition has been on tour from Egypt in the first decade of the twenty-first century. Perhaps future observers will see a new round of influence in the styles of the current decade.

Indian gurus were influential with Beatle George Harrison and others in the late 1960s and 1970s, so if the Maharajahs did not hold as much sway then as tastemakers, this newfound interest in another aspect of Indian culture may have opened the door to the use of large Indian style necklaces with Nehru collars or long, flowing clothes. The size and length of many of the necklace-pendants were not the only Indian motif that served as a source for jewelry that thrived in this cultural climate. Teardrop paisley shapes in bold colors, and coral, with both Indian and Middle Eastern forebears, found their way into 1960s and 1970s jewelry (figs. 27–31).

Designs with sources from around the world have continued to recur throughout VC&A's history. Japanese *inro* (fig. 32), a case for holding small objects, is invoked in a large gold compact with an engraved daisy pattern of 1950 (fig. 33). Indian embroidery inspired this 1970 necklace (fig. 34).

Despite the recurrence of some its exotic sources as fashions change, the jewelry of each age interprets its time rather than repeating the past. The fact that the Alhambra necklace has been in production for over forty years proves the continued appeal of a youthful interpretation from tradition and a testament to the ongoing appeal of adorning oneself with the exotic.

Fig. 23. Siamese Head brooch. New
York, NY, 1968. Yellow gold, rubies,
sapphires, emeralds, diamonds. Van
Cleef & Arpels' Collection

Fig. 25. Raja Playing Lute brooch. New York, NY, 1947. Yellow gold, rubies, emeralds, diamonds. Van Cleef & Arpels' Collection

Fig. 24. Goddess Head brooch. New York, NY, 1970. Gold, turquoise, rubies, emeralds, sapphires, diamonds. Courtesy of Richters of Palm Beach

Fig. 26. Egyptian pendant. New York, NY,
ca. 1970. Turquoise, ivory, yellow gold.
Van Cleef & Arpels' Collection

Fig. 27. Persian Leaf brooch. New York,
NY, 1966. Yellow gold, rubies, diamonds.
Van Cleef & Arpels' Collection

175

Fig. 28. Necklace with pendant and pair of earrings. Paris, France, 1972. Yellow gold, green and black onyx, coral, diamonds. Courtesy of Mrs. M. Elaine Crocker

Fig. 28. Necklace with pendant (detail)

Fig. 29. Venice Coral pair of bracelets
(combinable to form necklace) en suite
with pair of earrings. Paris, France, 1965.
Coral, diamonds, yellow gold. Van Cleef
& Arpels' Collection

Fig. 30. Venice Coral pair of earrings.
Paris, France, 1965. Coral, diamonds,
yellow gold. Van Cleef & Arpels'
Collection

Fig. 31. *Drapé* ring (part of a set, see
Transformations, p. 82). Paris, France,
1974. Yellow gold, coral, diamonds. Van
Cleef & Arpels' Collection

Fig. 32. Inro. Japan, 19th century.
Lacquer. Cooper-Hewitt, National
Design Museum, Smithsonian
Institution, Gift of Anonymous Donor,
1952-164-38

Fig. 33. Daisy compact. New York, NY,
1950. Yellow gold, diamonds. Van Cleef
& Arpels' Collection

Fig. 34. Indian Embroidery necklace. Paris, France, 1970. Yellow gold, rubies, emeralds, diamonds. Formerly owned by Princess Lilian of Belgium. Van Cleef & Arpels' Collection

Tassel sautoir. Paris, France, ca. 1930.
Turquoise, lapis lazuli, diamonds,
platinum. Courtesy of Private
Collection, New York

Monkey clock. Paris, France, 1926. Gold,
amethyst, onyx, amber. Van Cleef &
Arpels' Collection

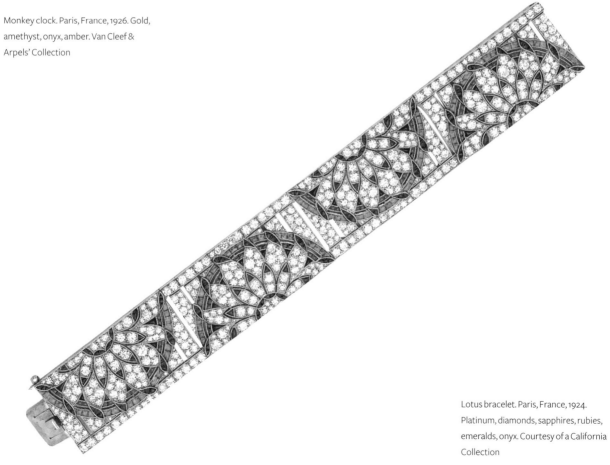

Lotus bracelet. Paris, France, 1924.
Platinum, diamonds, sapphires, rubies,
emeralds, onyx. Courtesy of a California
Collection

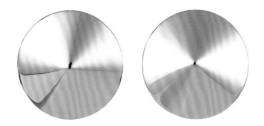

Chinese Hat pair of earrings and bracelet. Paris, France, 1931. Yellow gold. Van Cleef & Arpels' Collection

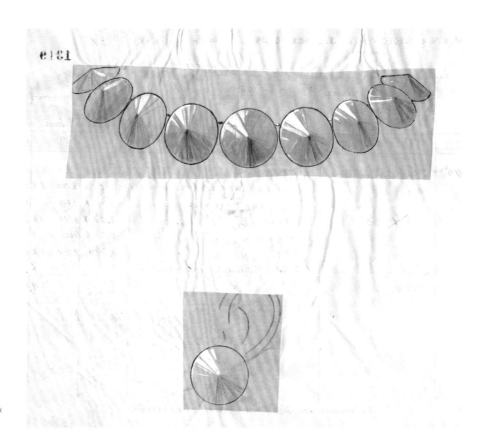

Book spread showing Chinese Hat necklace M37769. Paris, France, 1931. Gouache and ink on paper. Van Cleef & Arpels' Archives

Japanese Swords bracelet. Paris, France, 1958. Yellow gold, platinum, diamonds. Van Cleef & Arpels' Collection

Hawaii bracelet. New York, NY, 1945. Sapphires, diamonds, yellow gold. Van Cleef & Arpels' Collection

Dragon. Paris, France, ca. 1930. Gouache on paper. Van Cleef & Arpels' Archives

Ring and pair of earrings. New York, NY, 1975 and 1972. Yellow gold, carved coral, diamonds, emerald, green and black onyx. Courtesy of Carolyn Hsu-Balcer

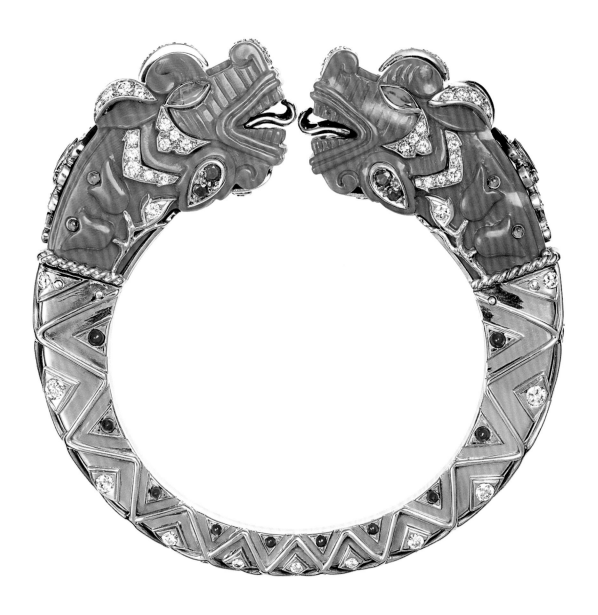

Dragon bracelet. New York, NY, 1974.
Diamonds, sapphires, coral, emeralds,
yellow gold. Courtesy of Private
Collection, United States

Brooch. New York, NY, 1972. Yellow
gold, ivory, carved pink tourmaline,
diamonds, emeralds. Van Cleef &
Arpels' Collection

Sultana ring. Paris, France, 1969. Yellow
gold, diamonds, sapphire, emeralds,
rubies. Van Cleef & Arpels' Collection

Necklace. Paris, France, 1957. Yellow gold, topaz, diamonds. Courtesy of Private Collection, New York

By Suzy Menkes

FASHION AND
VAN CLEEF & ARPELS

When women chopped off their hair and their hemlines in the 1920s, it could have spelled disaster for fine jewelry. How could the courtly diadem, nestling in upswept hair since the Belle Epoque, fit with the new short back and sides of the "garçonne," or boyish haircut? What was the future for diamond collars that blended with filigree lace bodices when Bright Young Things were dressed in simple tunics belted at the hips above daringly brief skirts?

Just as fashion holds up a mirror to changing times, so does jewelry, which has always followed the style of each century and the tone of the era—although it is often hard to judge whether clothing styles and jewels change simultaneously and symbiotically. But what is certain is that Van Cleef & Arpels was right on time when the house created the long, skinny necklaces called *sautoirs* (fig. 1) and the slender, graphic tiaras in the flapper years. Similarly, the jeweler made cuff-bracelets for bare-arm dresses in the 1930s and focused on romantic ballerinas when full skirts were symbolic of the postwar 1950s.

The links between fashion and jewelry—and between cloth and gems—have as many facets as a brilliant-cut diamond. First and foremost are the changes in style which, though not always immediately apparent, ultimately define a decade. A period piece is one that is recognizable as belonging to an era, and often a type of clothing. The duo of clips that were attached to corners of square-cut necklines in the late 1930s and 1940s are an example of a fashion in jewelry that followed the style of the times. Although the clips have since been worn in many other ways, that was their seminal moment.

No one could have predicted a devastating world war and the future emancipation of women when the Van Cleef and Arpels families united in 1896 and opened their first Paris boutique in 1906. Yet other factors for change were already in place. For example,

Art Deco powder compact. Paris, France, 1928. Gold, cabochon sapphires, blue and mauve enamel, diamonds. Van Cleef & Arpels' Collection

Fig. 1. Rivière necklace and clip. Paris, France, 1927. Platinum, diamonds. Courtesy of a California Collection

America had already seen the rise of barons of industry, who served up to jewelers their glamorous, young wives (and mistresses) free from conventional cultural and social constraints. The New World thus offered to Europe a bold attitude to color and style, just as in a previous era, connections with the colonies had inspired exotic styles.

One great fashion invention by VC&A, the Minaudière, a sculpted handheld purse, was inspired by Florence Jay Gould, wife of the American philanthropist Frank Jay Gould. The story has it that this modern-minded client of Charles Arpels met the jeweler with her belongings gathered into a Lucky Strike cigarette case made of tin. With French flair, Arpels translated this box in 1930 into a fabulous range of decorative vanity cases. It is significant that the "necessities" in the case were for a woman of the modern era, particularly those with the sporty, spirited American style: a comb to run through the fashionable bob; a case for lipstick (only recently accepted in high society); and cigarettes, the ultimate fashionable accessory (figs. 2, 3; see also Innovation, p. 26). Florence Gould was photographed in 1930 as a symbol of modern elegance: waved hair, pearl necklace, black fur stole, jeweled bracelet, and Minaudière.

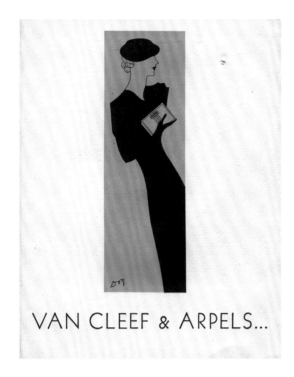

Fig. 2. Minaudière catalogue cover by Don. Paris, France, ca. 1930. Printed paper, foil. Van Cleef & Arpels' Archives

Fig. 3. Minaudière catalogue page spread. Paris, France, ca. 1930. Printed paper, foil. Van Cleef & Arpels' Archives

Fashion in the twentieth century can be viewed as the struggle for women to dress with the ease and simplicity that the tailored suit brought to men. The peacock male had long since jettisoned the velvet jackets, frilled shirts, embroidered vests, fancy breeches, and buckled shoes in favor of a sleeker wardrobe. The soul of VC&A is in the speed, energy, and "streamlining" that overtook the design world and liberated women's bodies from the corsetry emblematic of life in a gilded cage. Jewelry in the 1920s and 1930s had to be in tune with this sartorial emancipation (see frontispiece).

If fashion decades can be divided into the linear—like the long-line 1920s—and those drawn in the round, as in the 1950s, VC&A jewelry mirrored the geometry of the first part of the century. The 1925 *Exposition Internationale des Arts Décoratifs et Industriels Modernes* in Paris crystallized the concept of Art Deco, and brought jewelry that both complemented and helped define the style of the era. So the long, dangling earrings that went with the "garçonne" were also graphic in pattern (see Exoticism, p. 162). Jewels might have the metallic glint and sense of movement that reflected the new cars. Brooches were attached to the cloche hats that had replaced the extraordinary concoctions of Edwardian times. Pins were also worn on the shoulder or on the belt of a tunic. And the ultra-daring women who wore the first female tuxedos used geometric pins to decorate the lapels (figs. 4–6).

One of the fashion leaders was part of the jewelry family: Hélène Arpels, a former model for the Parisian couture firm House of Worth, who married Louis Arpels in 1933. This intrinsically glamorous woman lived between the United States and Paris, including fashionable vacation places such as Deauville and Cannes. The way she embraced fashion and understood how to embellish simple, well-cut clothes was a role model

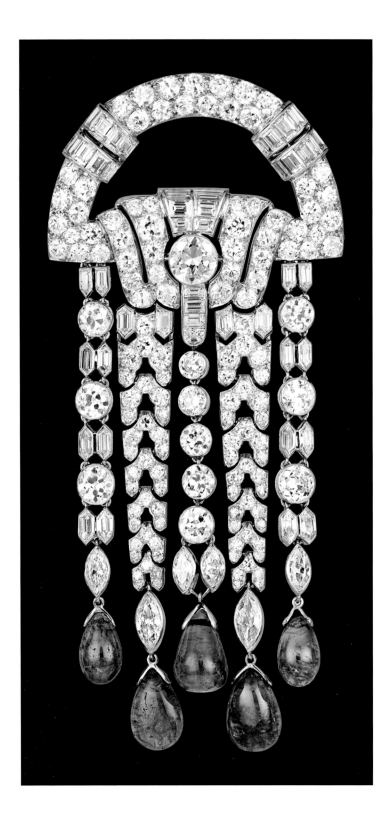

Fig. 5. *Art Deco Brooch Design no. 31364* retail card. Paris, France, 1927. Pigment and ink on card. Van Cleef & Arpels' Archives

Fig. 4. Art Deco brooch. Paris, France, 1928. Emeralds, diamonds, platinum. Formerly owned by Countess Hohenlohe. Van Cleef & Arpels' Collection

Fig. 6. Jabot brooch. Paris, France, 1925. Platinum, onyx, yellow gold, diamonds, emeralds. Van Cleef & Arpels' Collection

Fig. 7. Photo of Hélène Arpels, ca. 1938.
Van Cleef & Arpels' Archives

for burgeoning international society, including Daisy Fellowes, whose grandfather was the founder of Singer sewing machines, but whose society marriages put her on a higher plane. Hélène Arpels was a constant fixture on best-dressed lists, and not just for her choice of elegant outfits from her favorite couturier, Jean Patou. She had a way of wearing jewels, like her moveable diamond "flame" brooches from 1934, lining them up on her shoulder or even in her hair at the back. A photograph in the VC&A archives shows the former model as the incarnation of chic, with two clips at the high neckline of her plain black dress and a diamond bracelet on the cuff of the sleeve (fig. 7). The ribbon diamond brooch (fig. 8), which transforms into two separate clips, is a superb piece of craftsmanship from 1936, which was sold at Christie's 2006 auction of the Hélène Arpels collection in New York. The spray of overlapping pavé-set diamonds with a looped ribbon, mounted in platinum, has a luscious sensuality. Other exceptional pieces sold at the auction included a camellia brooch, a floral sculpture with oval-cut sapphire petals trimmed with diamonds, mounted on platinum and white gold.

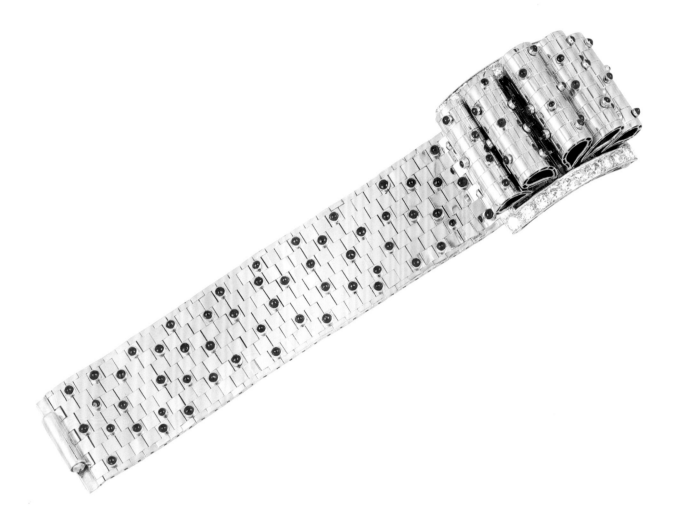

Fig. 9. Coques bracelet. Paris, France, 1936. Yellow gold, rubies, diamonds. Van Cleef & Arpels' Collection

Fig. 8. Double Pin Wave brooch. Paris, France, 1938. Platinum, diamonds. Van Cleef & Arpels' Collection

The most dramatic fashion change of the twentieth century came as women repudiated the straight-laced era of England's Queen Victoria, when a "glimpse of stocking was something shocking." Out too went the harsh, manmade colors that were part of the era's Industrial Revolution and the pale, powdery, ultra-feminine shades of Edwardian times. Instead, colors and patterns became more graphic in the 1920s, while soft tones like *eau de Nil*, or pale green, took over the elongated gowns in the 1930s. As hemlines lengthened and dresses became ultra-simple, society adopted fully bared arms for the first time since ancient Greece. The newly exposed area of flesh invited VC&A to reinvent bracelets and bangles, such as the 1939 diamond Ludo cuff (see Innovation, p. 37). Daisy Fellowes and fellow heiress Nancy Cunard became enthusiastic supporters of wide bracelets (fig. 9; also see Peltason, p. 246).

It is often imagined that the fashion duel of the era was played out by Gabrielle "Coco" Chanel, the proponent of casual clothes inspired by male hunting tweeds and polo field jersey, and her archrival, the surrealist Elsa Schiaparelli. Fellowes was one of "Schiap's" most faithful clients, appreciating the playful quality of her clothes that came from an

association with the work of Salvador Dalí. Yet it was other couturiers, such as Jeanne Lanvin, Maggie Rouff, and Madeleine Vionnet, who often created the clothes which formed the best backdrop for jewels. Dresses in the 1930s dissolved from sharp lines into graceful bias-cut drapery. Jewelry stayed in tandem, with a decline in geometry and a return to the figurative. Along with that came a move in jewelry mounting, from setting stones in icy platinum to the warmer yellow gold. The patenting of the *Serti mystérieux*, or "Mystery Setting," in 1933 only added to the mystique of VC&A and the sculptural feel of its jewels. The company's campaign advertising its new invention for curved surfaces showed the sleek silhouettes of 1930s women and the rounded surfaces of the mosaics of stones. The Peony brooch of 1937, its ruby petals opening over diamond leaves, one of the most extraordinary creations using the Mystery mounting, inspired a rage for this invention in fine jewelry (see Innovation, p. 11).

Fig. 10. Bronx Cocktail charm bracelet. Paris, France, 1937. Yellow gold, enamel, glass, colored stones. Van Cleef & Arpels' Collection

The multitude of jewels worn by Wallis Warfield Simpson, the Duchess of Windsor, caused a scandal in the late 1930s. No one knows for certain whether the cascade of gems that the future King Edward VIII showered on his married mistress was drawn from the royal collection or was the fruit of his trips to the India of the Maharajahs when he was Prince of Wales. What is certain is that VC&A made lavish pieces for the future king's twice-divorced American "friend," and when he gave her a sumptuous fortieth-birthday gift, he had the inside of the necklace engraved with the loving words: "My Wallis from her David, 19.06.1936." The necklace, with its tasseled tie of rubies and diamonds, was worn by the Duchess at their wedding in 1937, but altered by longtime VC&A designer René-Sim Lacaze in 1939 (see Peltason, p. 243). Accompanying the Windsor necklace was an articulated bracelet with four rectangles of ten rubies, separated by baguette and brilliant-cut diamonds. It captured the style of the 1930s, when the "brick" effects dominated bracelets such as the 1934 Ludo cuff, scattered with diamonds or the ruby "waves" in 1936. It is not surprising that, in an era when the "cocktail" was competing with dinner as smart entertainment, accessories included a bracelet of playful cocktail paraphernalia (fig. 10).

World War II changed everything. Even if the Depression era in the 1930s had put an end to flapper-girl frivolity, the magnitude of postwar upheaval affected every aspect of society. Schiaparelli and her witty touches went out of fashion, along with funky jewelry ideas such as Chinese hats creating a necklace, earrings, and ring (see Exoticism, p. 168). In the war, women were obliged to take over jobs vacated by men joining the military. The masculine clothes for working women required a different outlook and heavier jewelry to sit on the wide lapel of a tailored jacket. The defiant, bold, sculptural quality of the jewels distinguished them from the more delicate elegance of the 1930s. The war also inspired statements of love and hope, a yearning for family and for peace. Of all the jewels in the VC&A oeuvre, the clips of birds on a branch, a flaming torch (see Transformations, p. 99) or the word "pax" held in the beak of a bird, express most clearly the heartfelt spirit in hard times.

As the war ended, high fashion was in the doldrums and postwar Paris a wreck of its former architectural beauty. So the Chambre Syndicale de la Couture Parisienne, high fashion's ruling body, decided to make a concerted effort to promote the city's fashion image. In 1945, when Parisian women were drawing lines down the back of bared legs to pretend that they were wearing precious nylon stockings, an extraordinary group of figurines was created as the *Petit Théâtre de la Mode*, "Little Theater of Fashion." Two hundred tiny mannequins were dressed in miniature couture outfits by the great designers of the time. For the American tour of this fashionable world, magnificent,

Fig. 11. Rosace brooch. Paris, France, 1951. Diamonds, platinum. Courtesy of Private Collection

real jewels were added to give the finishing touches to the outfits. VC&A created a parure, or jewelry set, to capture the dramatic glamour of Schiaparelli's colorful satin Toreador dress. A tiny tiara of rubies and diamonds, set in platinum, was matched with epaulets for the wide 1940s shoulders, with a diamond and ruby bracelet used as a belt for the dress. The jewelry for couturier Maggie Rouff also featured a belt, but in a very different style. The soft dress, with its Grecian drapery, was caught at the waist with a long yellow gold cord, while a neckpiece and trio of bracelets were in sapphires and rubies set in yellow gold. The Petit Théâtre de la Mode was ultimately lost and forgotten—and rediscovered only in 1984, at the Maryhill Museum of Art in Goldendale, Washington—yet it served its purpose in the postwar period by reinvigorating high fashion and putting the focus back on Paris.

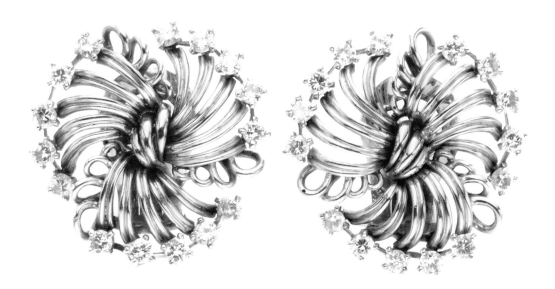

Fig. 12. Rosace pair of earclips. Paris, France, 1952. Yellow gold, platinum, diamonds. Courtesy of Private Collection

The 1950s marked the golden era of haute couture, and VC&A's collaborations with Cristobal Balenciaga showed the haughty glamour the firm was able to bring to the Spanish-born couturier's sensibility. Whether it was diamonds falling from a feathered hat in 1955 or a cluster of gems encircling the head behind a veil, Balenciaga found in the sophisticated jeweler the perfect partnership. The glossy magazines' great photographers of the postwar era made jewelry part of fashion-set pieces. The escapist beauty of the clothes created a similar effect as when Hollywood's silver screen stars of the 1930s offered an antidote to the Depression. In contrast to this icy couture elegance, however, jewelry in the 1950s featured a very different approach (figs. 11, 12). When the soldiers returned, hearth and home were at the heart of society, and popular jewelry of the 1950s picked up the mood of sweet romance—most especially in VC&A's dancing ballerinas with their bouncy skirts. The look, charmingly executed in polished rose gold or with encrustations of diamonds and emeralds, was the mirror image of popular fashion at that time. While high society wore structured suits and satin gowns, full skirts with paper nylon petticoats signaled on the streets that the dark days of the war were over (see Transformations, p. 95).

The link between fashion and jewelry may be set in precious stones. But there is another thread that binds imaginative jewelry to the world of style. It is literally the thread—as well as the cloth created from it. First and foremost, the process of haute couture and haute jewelry are similar, because both are about cutting and shaping, followed by mounting. Those ribbon necklaces are made to "fall" like cloth and often follow similar pieces of adornment, as in collars, cuffs, and bows (figs. 13–20). The bow is a recurring symbol both of the ties that bind a loving relationship and the strings that might hold a garment together. An enfolding ribbon, undulating across the finger, made a striking ribbon ring in 1945 (fig. 21).

Fig. 13. Serge Fabric necklace.New York, NY, 1953. Yellow gold, emeralds, diamonds. Van Cleef & Arpels' Collection

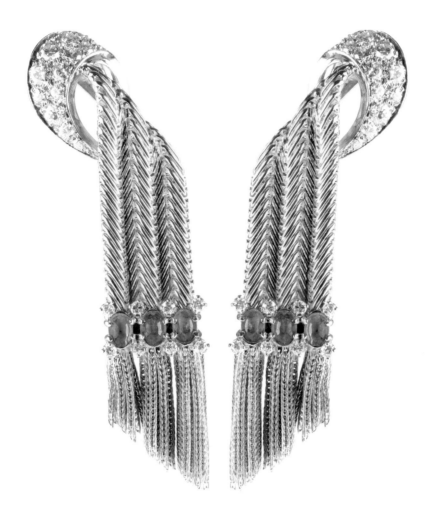

Fig. 14. Serge Fabric earrings. New York, NY, 1953. Diamonds, emeralds, yellow gold. Van Cleef & Arpels' Collection

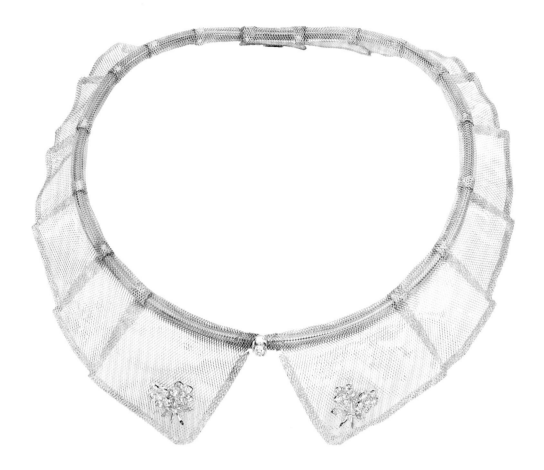

Fig. 15. Claudine collar necklace. Paris, France, 1983. Yellow gold, diamonds. Van Cleef & Arpels' Collection

The textures of fabric and the embellishment of cloth resonate in high jewelry (fig. 22). The delicate trellis of diamonds in the Belle Epoque was designed to resemble fashionable lace. The same idea was beautifully translated in VC&A's Art Deco bracelets, worked in diamonds with a grosgrain effect. Lace appeared again in a 1928 necklace (fig. 23) and in a 1964 diamond on platinum collar for Queen Sirikit of Thailand, while a tulle ring in 1940 captured the airy lightness of the material (fig. 24). What the French call *passementerie* and English speakers think of as the cording, braiding, and tassels most often associated with interior decoration has long been a source of inspiration for jewelry. Rivulets of tiny stones hanging in a cluster from a necklace emulated the tasselled closures for curtains in grand homes. Interesting texture and intriguing technique are often combined. In 1948, VC&A wittily named a braided necklace Couscous because it was made up of tiny grains, while the ultimate in "dressmaker" jewelry appeared three years later, in 1951, with a zipper necklace that actually slid open and closed like its more functional fashion version (see Innovation, p. 32, and Transformations, p. 71).

Embroidery is another perennial inspiration on jewelry, found as surface effects on boxes (fig. 25) and the Minaudières, where a lacquered box was decorated with a flower garden

Fig. 16. Brooch. New York, NY, 1956. Aquamarine, rubies, diamonds, platinum. Courtesy of Vartanian & Sons, Inc.

Fig. 17. Lace Bow brooch. Paris, France,
1949. Yellow gold, platinum, diamonds.
Van Cleef & Arpels' Collection

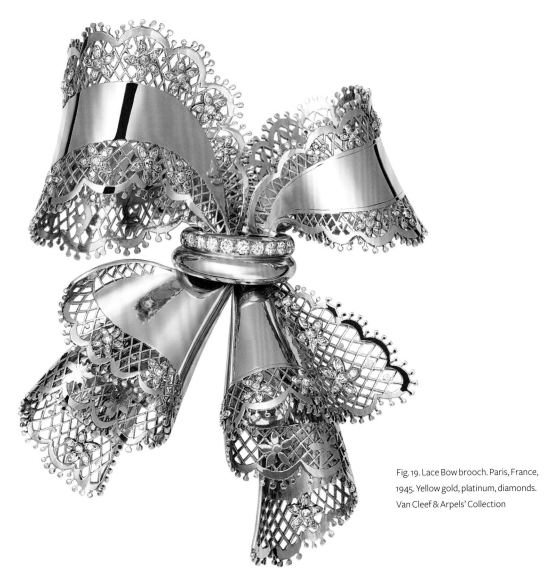

Fig. 19. Lace Bow brooch. Paris, France, 1945. Yellow gold, platinum, diamonds. Van Cleef & Arpels' Collection

Fig. 18. Page spread showing Lace bow brooch 62175. Paris, France, 1946. Gouache on paper. Van Cleef & Arpels' Archives

Fig. 20. *Lace Bow Brooch Design no. 55925* retail card. Paris, France, 1946. Pigment and ink on card. Van Cleef & Arpels' Archives

Fig. 21. Ribbon ring. Paris, France, 1945. Yellow gold, platinum, diamonds. Van Cleef & Arpels' Collection

Fig. 22. Basketweave purse. Paris, France, 1968. Yellow gold, diamonds. Courtesy of European Private Collection

of rubies in 1939. Other embroidery effects came on cloth evening bags with jeweled clasps from the 1920s and on a vanity case from 1925. The macramé or embroidery effect appeared as a vividly colored Indian-style necklace with turquoise flowers inset with diamonds and colored stones (fig. 26).

Fashion is often described as an eternal merry-go-round, and the Van Cleef & Arpels design spirit in jewelry has reappeared across the decades. When skirts fell in the 1970s, the sautoir made its return, along with the early Alhambra quatrefoils—the start of a necklace style that has become a continuing success story. The colorful strings were a perfect fit with the rock 'n' roll movement and the hippie era. The 1970s were also marked by a reprise of dangling tassels and by a different look at nature from the perennial flowers. Wood used for a necklace and ring (figs. 27, 28) suggested not only trees but also the worktables familiar to all creative studios.

Are fashionable lives and jewels still intertwined? The resurgence of the cocktail ring at the beginning of this new millennium can be seen as a response to the celebrity party era, while the red carpet and its uniform of strapless dresses and upswept hair has brought the big necklace and bold earrings back into the limelight. But the correlation between fashion and jewelry is above all about a feeling, a sensibility, and an emotional grasp of the decorative arts in ever-changing times, and throughout its long history, Van Cleef & Arpels has understood that link.

Fig. 23. Art Deco necklace. Paris, France, 1928. Diamonds, platinum. Van Cleef & Arpels' Collection

Fig. 24. Tulle ring. Paris, France, 1940.
Yellow gold, platinum, diamonds,
rubies. Van Cleef & Arpels' Collection

Fig. 25. Art Deco box. Paris, France, 1928.
Gold, engraved rock crystal, jadeite,
diamonds, onyx. Van Cleef & Arpels'
Collection

Fig. 26. Necklace. New York, NY, 1977.
Yellow gold, amethyst, turquoise,
diamonds. Courtesy of Anonymous
Lender

Fig. 27. Necklace. Paris, France, 1971.
Yellow gold, wood. Van Cleef & Arpels'
Collection

Fig. 28. Ring. Paris, France, 1970.
Yellow gold, wood. Van Cleef & Arpels'
Collection

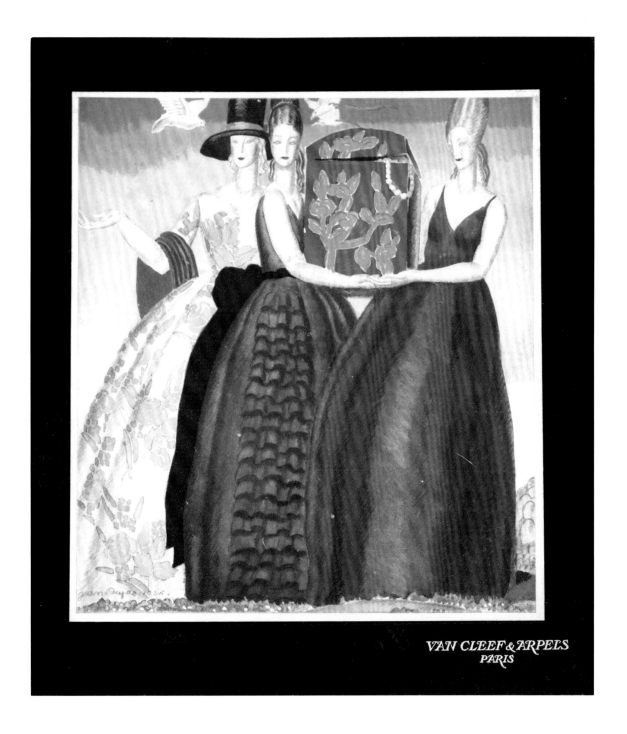

VAN CLEEF & ARPELS
PARIS

Catalogue cover by Jean Dupas. Paris,
France, 1925. Van Cleef & Arpels'
Archives

213

Art Deco powder case. Paris, France,
1936. Platinum, black lacquer, diamonds.
Van Cleef & Arpels' Collection

Envelope powder compact. Paris,
France, 1922. Yellow gold, white enamel.
Van Cleef & Arpels' Collection

Envelope powder compact. Paris,
France, 1923. Yellow gold, black
enamel, diamonds. Van Cleef & Arpels'
Collection

Bracelet. Paris, France, 1921. Sapphires, diamonds, platinum. Van Cleef & Arpels' Collection

216

Châtelaine watch. Paris, France, 1924.
Platinum, sapphires, diamonds, onyx,
enamel. Van Cleef & Arpels' Collection

Smoking (Dinner Jacket) watch. Paris, France, ca. 1930. White and yellow gold, enamel. Van Cleef & Arpels' Collection

Gadrooned wristwatch. Paris, France, ca. 1940. Yellow gold. Van Cleef & Arpels' Collection

Lighter. Paris, France, 1945. Yellow gold.
Van Cleef & Arpels' Collection

Batonnet cufflinks. New York, NY, 1969.
Rubies, gold. Courtesy of Neil Lane
Collection

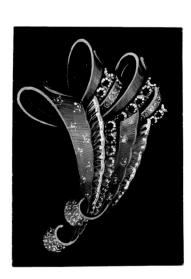

Flower brooches. Paris, France, ca.
1950. Gouache on paper. Van Cleef &
Arpels' Archives

Two Feathers brooch. Paris, France,
1954. Platinum, Mystery-Set sapphires,
diamonds. Van Cleef & Arpels'
Collection

Bouquet brooch. Paris, France, 1939.
Platinum, white and yellow diamonds.
Van Cleef & Arpels' Collection

Flot de ruban (Ribbon Wave) brooch.
Paris, France, 1937. Platinum, diamonds.
Formerly owned by Countess de
Beaurepaire. Van Cleef & Arpels'
Collection

Bow brooch. Paris, France, 1934.
Platinum, diamonds. Van Cleef & Arpels'
Collection

Cascades pair of earrings. Paris, France,
1951. Platinum, diamonds. Courtesy of a
California Collection

Art Deco evening bag. Paris, France,
1924. Platinum, seed pearls, diamonds.
Van Cleef & Arpels' Collection

Evening bag and circle clip. Paris, France, 1931. Diamonds, platinum, velvet. Van Cleef & Arpels' Collection

Circle brooch. Paris, France, 1931. Diamonds, platinum. Courtesy of Private Collection

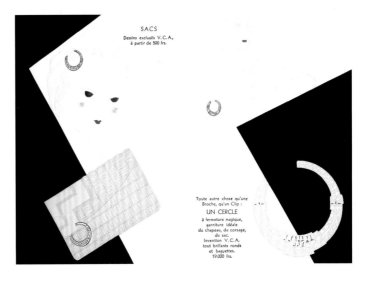

Advertisement for circle clip with collar, hat, and bag, ca. 1930. Van Cleef & Arpels' Archives

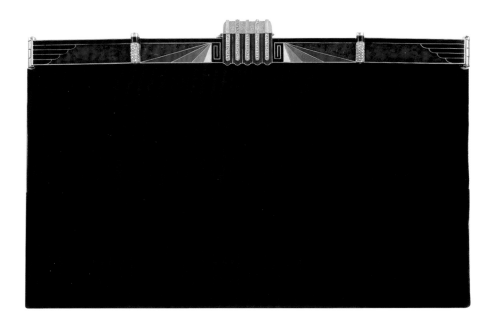

Evening bag. Paris, France, 1927.
Gold, black and blue enamel, rock
crystal, diamonds. Van Cleef & Arpels'
Collection

Evening bag. Paris, France, 1952. Yellow
gold, leather. Formerly owned by
Paulette Goddard. Courtesy of Private
Collection

Belle Hélène necklace. Paris, France, 1946. Yellow gold, diamonds, rubies. This model was worn by Catherine Deneuve in François Truffaut's film *Le Dernier Métro*. Van Cleef & Arpels' Collection

Manchette (cuff) bracelet. Paris, France, 1974. Yellow gold, lapis lazuli. Van Cleef & Arpels' Collection

By Ruth Peltason

BEJEWELED LIVES

Going back to the founding in Paris of Van Cleef & Arpels in 1906 and the opening of its New York boutique in 1939, the best-known and most beautiful women of the twentieth century have passed through the jeweler's welcoming doors—American heiresses and distinguished philanthropists; actresses and aristocrats; politicians and Social Register, all united by their inherent style and love of jewelry. They had the many elegant and worldly goods offered by VC&A: tiaras descended from Napoleon's wives, Josephine and Marie-Louise; necklaces and cuffs showcasing the vast coffers of fabulous emeralds owned by Indian royalty; an emerald-and-diamond engagement ring for a future First Lady; a sapphire-and-diamond Art Deco bracelet for an American newly ensconced as a duchess; a pearl-and-diamond suite intended for a royal bride of international acclaim and American birth; the Ludo, a golden honeycomb bracelet; the *jarretière*, a delicious scroll of rubies and diamonds; the Zip necklace and the Cadenas watch, ingenious adaptations of utilitarian hardware; clips of diamond bows, feathers, and flames; Mystery-Set holly leaves, peony, and poppy brooches; the Minaudière and the vanity case; Etruscan-style cuffs and the Alhambra necklace; butterflies that floated and hedgehogs that ambled. For more than a century, the remarkable history of Van Cleef & Arpels has been intertwined with the lives of many of the greatest personalities of our time. Each has enhanced the other and set the stage for the display of some of the grandest jewelry made in the twentieth century.

For Americans, the greatest ascent onto this world stage was embodied in Grace Kelly, she of the alluring smile and inner serenity, executed with her trademark perfect posture and constant composure. Her parents were both accomplished athletes, though for young Grace, with her "Breck girl" looks, it was acting, not sports, which led her to Hollywood. Once there, magic happened: the camera and Grace found one another. By the time she appeared in *Rear Window* (1954), Grace Kelly had gone from innocent to

Daisy brooch owned by H.S.H. Princess Grace of Monaco. Paris, France, 1956. Sapphires, diamonds, platinum. Private Collection of Her Serene Highness Princess Grace of Monaco, Principality of Monaco

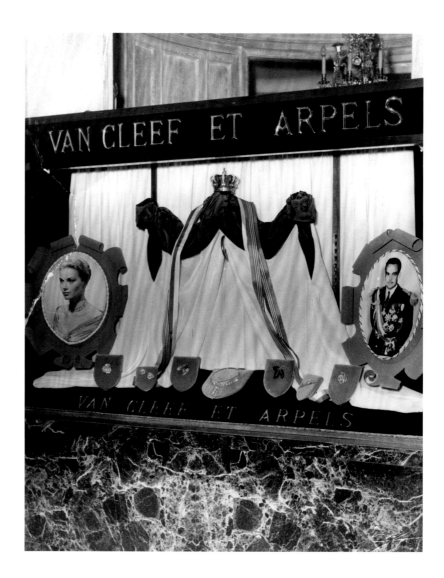

ingénue; *To Catch a Thief*, filmed a year later in Monaco, completed the transformation. Here was a white-gloved beauty who could purr like a kitten while seducing any man she wanted. On film it was Jimmy Stewart and Cary Grant; in real life, it was Prince Rainier III of Monaco. This Philadelphia-born girl traded in her Hollywood star for a lifelong role as Her Serene Highness Princess Grace of Monaco (fig. 1).

VC&A, designated the "Official Purveyor to the Principality," (fig. 2) made a pearl-and-diamond set for Prince Rainier's official engagement present in 1956 consisting of a necklace, bracelet, earrings, and ring (figs. 3a-d). Icy diamonds offset the creamy sensuous pearls, a natural pairing for a young bride and an apt symbol for the woman Alfred Hitchcock described as "a snow-covered volcano." Although the princess was presented with diamonds for her wedding, including a five-row diamond bracelet from Monaco's National and Municipal Council, her personal taste was quieter, wearable, more private citizen than public royal. She collected animal pins, including a poodle, a jeweled stand-in for her own pet poodle, Oliver. But the Alhambra necklace, with its quatrefoil

Figs. 3a–d. Engagement set: necklace,
bracelet (and detail), earrings, ring for
H.S.H. Princess Grace of Monaco. New
York, NY, 1956. Diamonds, cultured
pearls, platinum. Private collection of
Her Serene Highness Princess Grace of
Monaco, Principality of Monaco

233

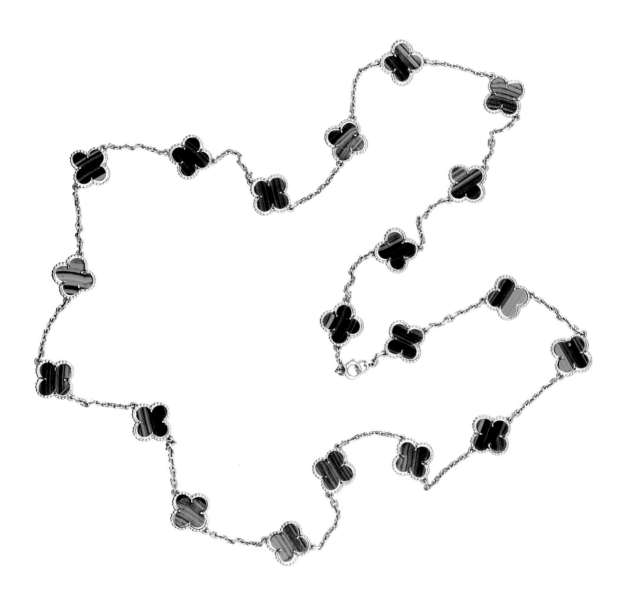

Fig. 4. Alhambra necklace owned by
H.S.H. Princess Grace of Monaco. Paris,
France, 1975. Yellow gold, malachite.
Private collection of Her Serene
Highness Princess Grace of Monaco,
Principality of Monaco

motif recalling Moorish architecture, is most identified with Kelly, who owned several of
the necklaces (fig. 4). When VC&A introduced it in 1968, the Alhambra collection quickly
became a beacon of privilege, its distinctive four-leaf clover shape filled variously with
malachite, lapis, tortoiseshell, mother-of-pearl, wood, and diamonds.[2] Years later, in
her role as mother of the bride, Her Serene Highness Princess Grace donned one of the
emblems of her title, a diamond tiara made by VC&A, which she wore to the wedding of
her elder daughter, Princess Caroline, in 1978 (fig. 5).

Although Kelly is the only actress who permanently crossed into royalty, Hollywood has
long had a romance with Van Cleef & Arpels, going back to early screen stars Greta Garbo,
Gloria Swanson, and Marlene Dietrich. The Berlin-born Dietrich, famously described
by writer Erich Maria Remarque as "a steel orchid," was the owner of many fine pieces
of VC&A jewelry, including a pair of gold lace ear clips set with sapphires and diamonds
(1948), a three-strand pearl choker with platinum and diamond plaques (1949), and a
vanity case (1962). Most notable by far was a sumptuous ruby-and-diamond platinum
jarretière, made with her own jewels.[3] (fig. 6) This magnificent cuff, whose creation she

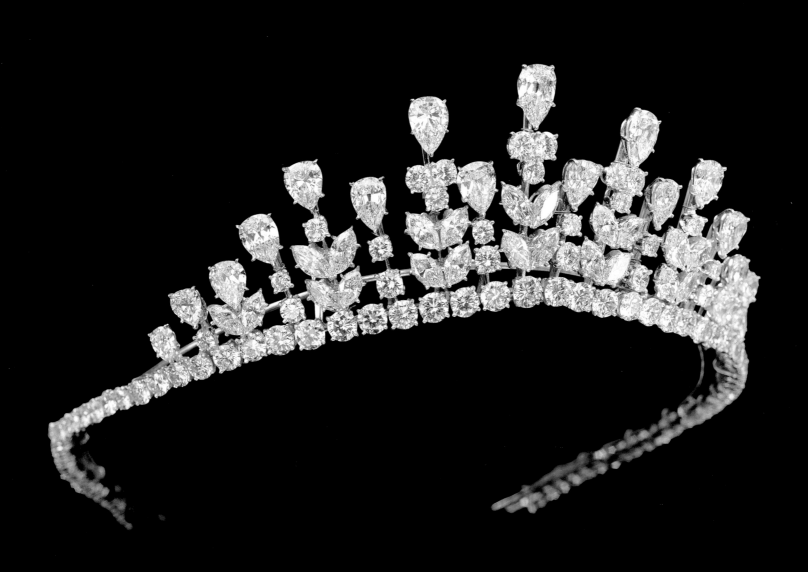

Fig. 5. Tiara worn by H.S.H. Princess
Grace of Monaco for the wedding of
Princess Caroline in 1978. Paris, France,
1976. Diamonds, gold, platinum. Van
Cleef & Arpels' Collection

Fig. 6. *Jarretière* bracelet formerly
owned by Marlene Dietrich. Paris,
France, ca. 1937. Rubies, diamonds,
platinum. Courtesy of Private
Collection, New York

Fig. 7. Marlene Dietrich and Richard
Todd in the film *Stage Fright* directed
by Alfred Hitchcock, April 22, 1950.
Photo by Picture Post/Hulton Archive/
Getty Images

consulted on with Louis Arpels, dates from 1937, and according to her grandson Peter
Riva, was "the only piece of jewelry she kept."[4] Surprisingly, the bracelet was only seen
intermittently—at the swanky Bal des Petits Blancs children's fundraiser in Cannes in 1938,
with more than 1,700 guests in attendance,[5] and onscreen in Alfred Hitchcock's *Stage
Fright* (1950) (fig. 7), after which Dietrich returned it to her vault and never wore it again.
It did not appear again until four decades later, at auction in October 1992, five months
after the star's death.[6]

Fig. 8. Band ring formerly owned
by Greta Garbo. New York, NY, 1949.
Diamonds, platinum. Courtesy of
Private Collection

Whereas Dietrich was all legs and smoky seduction, Garbo made an art of being
unattainable, onscreen and off. Known as "the face" or "the Swedish sphinx," Garbo's
mysterious demeanor was a lifelong mirage. From Van Cleef & Arpels, one of her major
purchases of jewelry was a large diamond ring of nearly ten carats, as cool and gorgeously
faceted as the Nordic beauty herself.[7] (fig. 8)

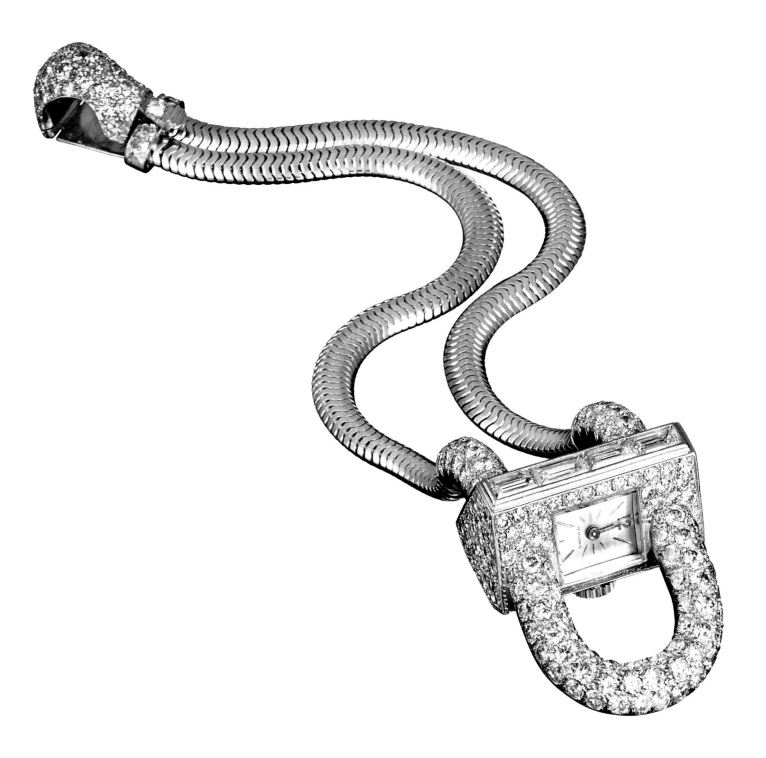

Fig. 9. Cadenas (padlock) watch
formerly owned by Paulette Goddard.
New York, NY, 1940. Diamonds,
platinum. Van Cleef & Arpels'
Collection

Paulette Goddard, star of such vehicles as *Modern Times* (1936) and *The Great Dictator* (1940), featuring her husband Charlie Chaplin, and *The Women* (1939), was famous for her love of jewelry.[8] With her ready wit and striking looks, Goddard acquired jewelry only slightly more than she acquired husbands, including, from VC&A, a stunning padlock-style Cadenas gold watch (fig. 9), a brooch from its Snowflake collection, a 1960s cabochon ruby-and-diamond necklace which converted into a bracelet, and a suite of yellow and blue sapphire-and-ruby clips, earrings, and ring.[9]

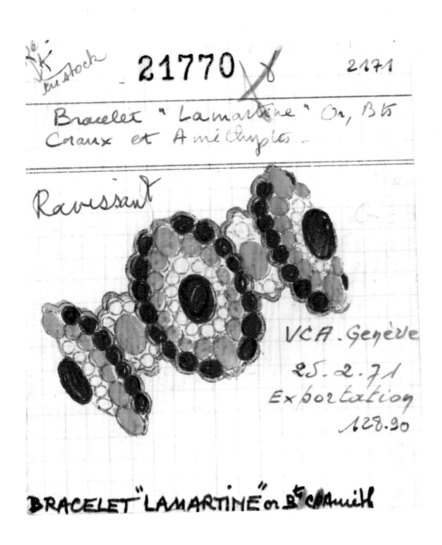

Fig. 10. *Lamartine bracelet design no. 21770* retail card. Paris, France, ca. 1970. Pigment and ink on card. Van Cleef & Arpels' Archives

When it comes to greatness of reputation, beauty, and collection, there has been no brighter light in Hollywood than Elizabeth Taylor. By the time she made *Cleopatra* (1963), her dazzling star had collided with Richard Burton's, a romantic explosion that laid the foundation for one of the best private jewelry collections in the United States. Burton had a natural eye for jewelry, and the two actors were frequent customers of VC&A's ateliers worldwide.[10] On one excursion, Burton bought his wife an extraordinary 8.90-carat ruby-and-diamond ring, and in Geneva, in February 1971,[11] he purchased the "Lamartine," a bracelet of diamonds, coral, and amethyst (to play on her dramatically colored violet eyes), along with matching ear pendants (figs. 10, 11a, 11b). A year later, the Burtons attended the Proust Ball, given by the Baron and Baroness Guy de Rothschild at the Château de Ferrières, in Seine-et-Marne, France, where the dress code required the

Figs. 11a, 11b. Lamartine bracelet and pair of pendant earrings owned by Elizabeth Taylor. Paris, France, 1970 and 1971. Amethyst, coral, diamonds, platinum, yellow gold. Courtesy of Dame Elizabeth Taylor. Photography by John Bigelow Taylor

women to have bejeweled hairstyles. For the event, VC&A loaned Taylor several pieces of diamond jewelry to approximate a diadem.[12] (fig. 12) Over the years, Dame Elizabeth has continued to add Van Cleef & Arpels to her collection, including a magnificent Art Deco Bow Knot brooch (ca. late 1926) and a pair of Mystery-Set sapphire-and-diamond ear pendants (figs. 13, 14).

The Burtons were friendly with the Duke and Duchess of Windsor, and the Duchess shared Dame Elizabeth's love of fine jewelry. The Duke, formerly Prince Edward and, for eleven months, Edward VIII, King of England, had the instincts of a dandy (fig. 15) and the manners of his royal lineage, which combined to make for some especially amusing and spectacular gifts to his wife. Prior to their marriage, and notably on their wedding day, June 3, 1937, the Duchess wore jewelry made by VC&A that had been chosen by the Duke. On that day, at the Château de Condé, outside of Paris, the Duchess wore two stunning sapphire-and-diamond pieces: a geometric-style clip comprising eleven faceted sapphires, diamond baguettes, and brilliants, pinned at the neck of her Mainbocher blue satin dress, and a *jarretière* of Mystery-Set cushion-shaped sapphires and diamonds, often referred to as the Windsor's "contract" bracelet, because of its inscription, "For our contract 18-V-37." The Duke was forever spoiling his wife with jewelry, and from VC&A that often meant rubies and diamonds, such as a pair of Mystery-Set ruby-and-diamond ear clips; a ruby-and-diamond bracelet of four rectangular *bombé* links set with cushion-shaped rubies, inscribed "Hold Tight 27-iii-36" (1936); and the Duke's gift to his wife on her fortieth birthday, the "Tie" necklace of rubies and diamonds of *entrelac-de-rubans* design (1936, redesigned 1939).[13] (fig. 16)

By the 1920s, American society had designated New York, Newport, Palm Beach, London, and Paris as places to meet and mingle, with jaunts to more exotic locales in India and Mexico. For Natasha and Jacques Gelman, who later became important art collectors,[14] Mexico was paradise. Russian-born Jacques, a successful film producer, and his vivacious wife were well liked and outgoing, and befriended such artists as Frida Kahlo, Diego Rivera, and Alfaro Siqueiros. From Rivera they commissioned the painting *Portrait of Mrs. Natasha Zakalkowa Gelman* (1943, private collection). Natasha looks out at us while reclining, odalisque-style, on a pile of cushions, surrounded by large calla lilies, their shape echoed in the sensuous opening of her dress (fig. 17). For the jewelry maven, the cool glow from her left wrist commands attention: a platinum-and-diamond Ludo bracelet, which her husband bought sometime after their marriage in 1941 (fig. 18).

Fig. 12. Elizabeth Taylor dressed for the Proust Ball in *Vogue*, February 1972. Diadem composed of Taylor's own jewelry and pieces loaned by VC&A. Cecil Beaton / Vogue © The Condé Nast Publications Ltd.

Fig. 13. Art Deco Bow Knot brooch owned
by Elizabeth Taylor. Paris, France, 1926.
Diamonds, platinum. Courtesy of Dame
Elizabeth Taylor. Photography by John
Bigelow Taylor

Fig. 14. Mystery-Set Drop pair of
pendant earrings owned by Elizabeth
Taylor. New York, NY, 1984, pendants
1985. Sapphires, diamonds, platinum.
Courtesy of Dame Elizabeth Taylor.
Photography by John Bigelow Taylor

Fig. 15. Set of cufflinks formerly owned
by the Duke of Windsor. Paris, France,
1928. Sapphires, diamonds, platinum.
Van Cleef & Arpels' Collection

Also by this time, "American heiress" was parlance for a specific kind of female independence, fueled by family money. For many of these Americans, Paris was like a second home where they entertained, shopped the great couture houses, and called on Van Cleef & Arpels at 22, place Vendôme, where the jeweler offered quality, taste, discretion, and the personal attention of Louis and Claude Arpels. Heiress Daisy Fellowes, born in the City of Lights in 1890, was known for her singular style, which Cecil Beaton described as "studied simplicity"—words that could be applied to her jewelry as well.[15] She owned two magnificent Indian-style diamond bracelets dating from the 1920s (fig. 19). Purchased in 1926 and 1928, they were sumptuous compositions of baguette, brilliant, and marquise-cut diamonds, fringed with emeralds, which she would wear on each wrist (figs. 20, 21). They were also made to be combined and worn as a dramatic *collier de chien* (dog collar). How not to overwhelm those grand VC&A *manchettes*? By downstaging the clothes, which in her case might have meant wearing an elegantly cut satin gown as a neutral backdrop.[16] In the late 1920s, she was also given another similarly styled cuff, with a ruby fringe. Fellowes also had an Art Deco bracelet (1925), a hexagonal Ludo bracelet and matching earrings (1936), and a diamond ring of 17.90 carats (1925).

Fig. 16. *Windsor Necklace*. Paris, France, 1936. Gouache on paper. This is the Duchess of Windsor's necklace as first designed by René-Sim Lacaze, who updated it in 1939. Van Cleef & Arpels' Archives

Fig. 17. *Portrait of Mrs. Natasha Zakalkowa Gelman* by Diego Rivera (Mexican, 1886-1957), 1943. Oil on canvas. © 2010 Banco de México Diego Rivera Frida Kahlo Museums Trust, Mexico, D.F. / Artists Rights Society (ARS), New York

Although many Americans came to seek the hedonistic life in Paris, one arrival in particular distinguished herself. She was born Florence La Caze, but it was the married name of Gould that gave this former opera singer and amateur water skier currency in social circles, especially in the Côte d'Azur, where she and her husband, Frank Jay Gould, son of the American railroad magnate, Jay Gould, lived in great expatriate splendor.[17] The Riviera had been a winter resort prior to the Goulds' arrival in the mid-1920s, but they transformed the dozy coastal area into an exclusive playground for the wealthy, the literary, and much of Hollywood. Frank Jay Gould built a hugely profitable casino, the Palais de la Mediterranée, an Art Deco pile in Nice, and retooled an existing one in Juan-les-Pins, making the village an instant destination for the likes of Scott and Zelda Fitzgerald.[18] In Paris, at their apartment on the avenue Malakoff, Florence Gould was hostess of a literary salon that included André Gide, Jean Cocteau, and Salvador Dalí. She was already a devoted VC&A client when she served as the inspiration for the jeweler's enchanting Minaudière, a lavishly decorated daytime case (see Innovation, p. 26, and fig. 22). Where the Minaudière was all quiet glamour, there was nothing subtle about Florence Gould's "Blue Princess" stone, also known as the "Neela Ranee." While on a buying trip to India in 1956, Claude Arpels had acquired the extraordinary 114-carat

Fig. 18. Ludo Hexagon bracelet formerly owned by Natasha Gelman. Paris, France, 1939. Diamonds, platinum. Van Cleef & Arpels' Collection

blue sapphire from a dealer in Bombay (today Mumbai). Less than a decade later, Gould purchased it and had it placed as the central motif in a necklace of legendary beauty, surrounded by three other significant blue sapphires and diamonds. Gould had many other significant VC&A pieces, including an emerald-and-diamond bracelet with five rectangular-cut emeralds alternating with four rectangular-cut diamonds; an angelfish sapphire-and-diamond brooch, set with a star sapphire of approximately 179.49 carats; and an Art Deco pearl compact of 1925.[19] The latter is a lesson in the art of the simple: the black lacquer case serves as the elegant foundation for more than 900 natural pearls, further enhanced with the addition of 130 diamonds (fig. 23).

For Marjorie Merriweather Post, the only child of Post cereal founder C. W. Post, money truly was no object: by the time of her death in 1973 her estate was worth $200 million, or nearly four times that in today's dollars (fig. 24). A fervent collector, Post acquired eighty objects made by Fabergé, including two Imperial Easter eggs—part of her stellar collection of Russian artworks, the best of its kind outside of Russia, even today—as well as priceless Sèvres porcelain and other renowned French decorative arts. The same informed decisions and search for quality also made her a discerning collector

Fig. 19. Socialite Daisy Fellowes
wearing *manchette* bracelets, London,
December 7, 1934. © Bettmann/
CORBIS

Fig. 20. *Manchette (cuff) bracelet
design no. 31254* retail card. Paris,
France, 1926. Pigment and ink on card.
Van Cleef & Arpels' Archives

Fig. 21. *Manchette (cuff) bracelet /
necklace* formerly owned by Daisy
Fellowes. Paris, France, 1926. Emeralds,
diamonds, platinum. Courtesy of a
California Collection

Fig. 22. Lattice nécessaire powder
compact formerly owned by Florence
Gould. Paris, France, 1925. Seed
pearls, black enamel, diamonds, white
gold, platinum. Van Cleef & Arpels'
Collection

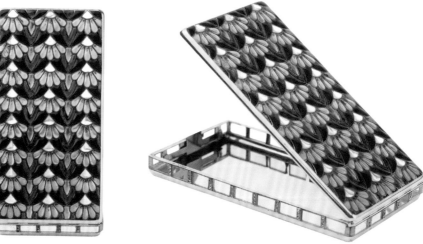

Fig. 23. Nécessaire formerly owned by
Florence Gould. Paris, France, 1925. Red,
green, yellow and blue enamel, yellow
gold. Van Cleef & Arpels' Collection

Fig. 24. Marjorie Merriweather Post at
the Red Cross Ball. Palm Beach, 1967.
Hillwood Estate, Museum & Gardens
Archives

of fine jewelry, especially from Van Cleef & Arpels (fig. 25). For the Palm Beach Red
Cross International Gala of 1970, held at her lavish Mar-a-Lago estate, which included a
62,500-square-foot house with 115 rooms, she borrowed from the jeweler its Empress
Marie-Louise tiara, one of three historic jewels they owned known as Napoleon's
Court.[20] The tiara, whose design is attributed to Etienne Nitot et fils, the official jewelers
to Napoleon, originally consisted of twenty-two large emeralds, including a square-cut
emerald in the centerpiece weighing twelve carats, and as many as 500 diamonds. In the
late 1950s and early 1960s, VC&A sold the emeralds to discerning clients and replaced
them with Persian turquoise stones; a year later, Post purchased the tiara and donated
it to the Smithsonian Institution.[21] Another of her donations to the nation's museum

complex is the incomparable "Blue Heart," a blue diamond of 30.82 carats, in a league with two other major blue diamonds, the Wittelsbach Blue and the Hope Diamonds, the latter also at the Smithsonian. The Blue Heart, which dates back to 1908, was purchased by VC&A in 1953, when it was displayed as a pendant necklace valued at $300 million. It was later sold to Harry Winston, which made it into a ring; Post purchased the ring in 1964. VC&A made a number of floral brooches with Mystery-Set rubies and diamonds, including one owned by the cereal heiress from 1967 (fig. 26). Others included a peony brooch (1937), formerly owned by Mahmoud Fakhry Pacha of Egypt; a poppy brooch (1956); a sugar maple leaf clip with faceted rubies and diamonds (1967), owned by the great opera diva Maria Callas; as well as the Double Holly brooch (1937), owned by the Duchess of Windsor, who wore it pinned to an evening gown or jacket and, more strikingly, in her hair.

Post will always be remembered for her great philanthropy, which also distinguished Doris Duke, who gave away the equivalent of $400 million over eight decades. Dubbed "the richest little girl in the world" at birth in 1912, she was an arresting, if not classical,

Fig. 26. Flower brooch owned by
Marjorie Merriweather Post. Paris,
France, 1967. Rubies, diamonds, yellow
gold, platinum. Hillwood Estate,
Museum & Gardens; Bequest of Marjorie
Merriweather Post, 1973. Photo :
E. Owen

Fig. 27. Doris Duke Cromwell and James
Cromwell at Shangri-La, 1939/1940.
Doris Duke Photograph Collection,
Doris Duke Charitable Foundation
Historical Archives, Rare Book,
Manuscript, and Special Collections
Library, Duke University

Figs. 28a-c. Hawaii bracelet, ring, and
pair of earrings formerly owned by
Doris Duke. Paris, France, 1938 and
1953 (earrings). Sapphires, rubies,
diamonds, platinum, yellow gold.
Courtesy of Hazel Shanken

beauty with widely set eyes and an imposing height of six feet (fig. 27). But for all her
assets, she was doomed to heartbreak in her personal life, beginning with the demise of
her first marriage, in 1935, to James Cromwell while on their honeymoon. She married
one other time, to Porfirio Rubirosa, a notorious Dominican playboy and politician, but
had many lovers, including Errol Flynn and General George Patton. One of her first lovers,
British MP Alec Cunningham-Reid, gave her a bracelet and ring from VC&A's Hawaii floral
collection when it was launched in 1938—a fitting gift since she had recently built a five-
acre estate, Shangri-La, on Honolulu, near Diamond Head (figs. 28a–c). As depicted by
René-Sim Lacaze, chief designer for Van Cleef & Arpels, the stylized forget-me-nots of
the Hawaii line were shown in the French patriotic colors of red, white, and blue—rubies,
diamonds, and sapphires, respectively, symbolic as *"les petites fleurs de la résistance."*[22]
In 1953, Duke commissioned the jeweler to make her a pair of matching earrings as well.
An instinctive collector, she also acquired Southeast Asian and Islamic art on her many
travels. India was most dear to her, and over time Duke purchased an excellent trove
of Indian Mughal jewelry. Duke's flair for redesigning jewelry further distinguished her
collection. There was, for instance, her gold Ludo bracelet: the clasp had diamonds and
carved-fish sapphires and rubies, originally made in India and purchased there by Duke's
mother.[23]

Fig. 29. Art Deco bracelet formerly
owned by the Duchess of Marlborough
(née Consuelo Vanderbilt). Paris, France,
1925. Sapphires, diamonds, platinum. Van
Cleef & Arpels' Collection

Fig. 30. Knot brooch, owned by the
Marquesa de Cuervas (née Margaret
Rockefeller Strong). Paris, France,
1955. Diamonds, platinum. Van Cleef &
Arpels' Collection

Marrying aristocrats seemed to appeal to many American women born into wealth, and they also looked to Van Cleef & Arpels jewelry to enhance their stature. As the Duchess of Marlborough, the former Consuelo Vanderbilt owned an Art Deco bracelet of sapphires, diamonds, and platinum (1925) (fig. 29). Anna Gould, who became the Comtesse de Castellane, had one of the jeweler's châtelaine watches in black and green enamel (1924); and Margaret Strong, a Rockefeller on her mother's side[24] who married the Marquis de Cuevas, a Chilean businessman with a passion for ballet, owned an especially simple but expressive diamond bow made in 1955 (fig. 30).

Of course, neither matrimony nor money means happiness. When it comes to claims
of unhappiness associated with great wealth, that dubious distinction settles on the
shoulders of Barbara Hutton. Her grandfather was F. W. Woolworth and her father was
F. L. Hutton, a co-founder of the eponymous investment-banking firm; and she was
a niece by marriage of Marjorie Merriweather Post, whose second husband was E. F.
Hutton. Misfortune arrived by the time Hutton was five, when her mother committed
suicide. In 1925, when Noel Coward wrote the lyrics for "Poor Little Rich Girl," Hutton
and the song became forever entwined—"The life you lead sets all your nerves a-jangle/
Your love affairs are in a hopeless tangle/...Cocktails and laughter, But what comes after?"
Although Hutton had seven husbands, including Cary Grant and Porfirio Rubirosa
(Doris Duke preceded her in this regard by six years),[25] she was best known for her vast
collection of jewelry. It featured pieces of great historic value and importance, such as
the Pasha diamond, originally an octagon of forty carats and at one time owned by King
Farouk (r. 1936–52), and an emerald tiara containing seven important emeralds, once
owned by the Grand Duchess Vladimir and purchased by VC&A in 1965 (fig. 31). Pearls
were a signature style, beginning at her debutante party when her father gave her a single
strand of pearls supposedly owned by Marie-Antoinette and valued at the astronomical
price of $1 million.[26] It is tempting to list jewelry when it comes to Barbara Hutton, for she
bought often and in vast quantities (figs. 32, 33). In 1943, as Mrs. Cary Grant, she bought

Fig. 32. Ludo bracelet formerly owned
by Barbara Hutton. Paris, France, 1935.
Platinum, diamonds. Van Cleef & Arpels'
Collection

a Minaudière, its tidy interior compartments filled with a gold-and-sapphire lipstick holder, vanity case, and gold-and-sapphire cigarette case with matching lighter. Around the same time, she purchased a darling pin, the Dragonfly Fairy brooch (fig. 34). The jeweler produced various Fairy pins in the 1940s, but Hutton's is both daintier and more svelte than the others. She also admired their newly introduced ballerina brooches,[27] purchasing one in 1943 comprising emeralds, rubies, and sapphires, and again in 1946, this one with an allover gold-and-turquoise skirt and a posy of ruby flowers. For Christmas 1946, she had VC&A send scores of brooches, cufflinks, and watches to friends and business associates, and in February 1947 she purchased an emerald-and-diamond bracelet.[28] To mark the end of World War II, Van Cleef & Arpels issued a peace brooch, which she acquired. Two stellar purchases came later: in 1966, as Princess Doan Vinh na Champassak, she bought a ring set with an 18.86-carat ruby and twenty-two diamonds of 9.13 carats, and in 1970, an all-diamond tiara, with a ticket price of $1.08 million.[29] According to company archives, the tiara had twenty-two pear-shaped diamonds of 119.89 carats, including three pear-shaped navettes weighing 54.82, 21.49, and 21.62 carats; fifty-eight navettes of 58.91 carats; and 127 brilliants weighing 42.84 carats.[30]

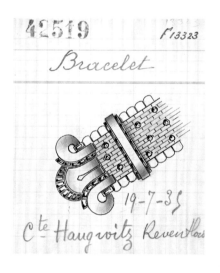

Fig. 33. *Ludo bracelet design no. 42519* retail card. Paris, France, 1935. Pigment and ink on card. Van Cleef & Arpels' Archives

By the 1960s, a new kind of American style icon had confidently stepped into the limelight—Jacqueline Kennedy. Like Doris Duke, she had widely set features, though hers were softer and prettier; and like Florence Jay Gould she was athletic, but her turf was the horse ring, not the ocean; and though she was raised in genteel comfort, she married what was even bigger in American terms: the man who became the thirty-fifth U.S. President, John F. Kennedy. Their relationship was an alliance of power and beauty, grace and style, consecrated with an emerald-and-diamond engagement ring that then-Senator Kennedy purchased from Van Cleef & Arpels in the summer of 1953. Jacqueline Kennedy eschewed traditional tiaras in favor of a lighter glimmer, as when she wore VC&A diamond Wheat Sheaf and Flame clips[31] in her hair to a dinner given by President and Madame de Gaulle at Versailles on June 1, 1961, accenting a Givenchy hand-embroidered ivory silk dress.[32] (figs. 35, 36) The impression she made at this red-letter dinner prompted the now-famous remark by President Kennedy, "I am the man who accompanied Jacqueline Kennedy to Paris."[33] From her second husband, Aristotle Onassis, she received exquisite VC&A jewelry, including an emerald-and-diamond necklace consisting of pear-shaped emeralds of 132 carats as one of her engagement presents as well as a cabochon

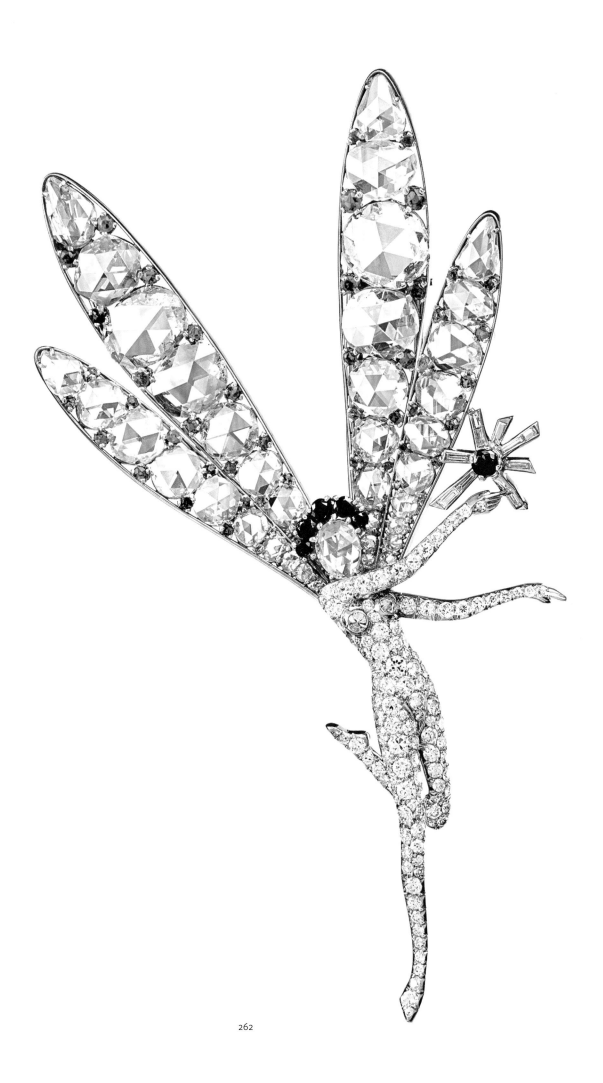

emerald ring of 61.17 carats surrounded by diamonds. Given her overall restrained style of dress as she got older, she preferred less wattage in her jewelry (fig. 37), especially when it was in gold and ethnic in style. From VC&A, for instance, she owned a pair of gold flattened hoop earrings (ca. 1972) and a pair of Etruscan-style hammered gold cuffs (1973) (fig. 38).

It was in India where one of the great stories of jewelry collections involving power, intrigue, and a beautiful, commanding woman came to life. When Sita Devi, a captivating figure, met her future second husband, Maharajah Pratapsinghrao Gaekwad of Baroda, in 1943, both were already married. But the attraction was powerful enough that the Maharajah divorced his first wife and married Sita Devi, who became the new Maharani of Baroda. Her unofficial title, anointed in the press, was the "Indian Wallis Simpson." (In fact, the two women once met at a grand party, with less-than-happy results, especially for the Duchess.[34]) For Sita Devi, marriage brought enormous riches—the Maharajah was reputed to be the eighth richest man in the world, with an estimated yearly income of $8 million[35]—including some of the most sumptuous jewelry known at that time, especially the peerless seven-strand Baroda natural pearls, a pearl-encrusted carpet, and a necklace with the 128.80-carat Star of the South diamond suspending a pendant of the English Dresden diamond of 78.53 carats.

Not long after the Indian Independence of 1947, Claude and Jacques Arpels went to India, where they called on various rulers and purchased important jewels. In 1949, the Maharani commissioned the jewelers to make her the "Hindu Necklace" or "Lotus Necklace," made of thirteen pear-shaped Colombian emerald drops weighing a total of 150 carats, suspended from pavé-set diamonds in the shape of a lotus flower (figs. 39, 40a, 40b). The magnificent design was paired with ear pendants of octagonal and drop-shaped emeralds and briolette diamonds. Remarkably, all of the stones came from the Maharani herself. She remained an important client of Van Cleef & Arpels and her collection included at least two other pairs of emerald-and-diamond earrings commissioned from them: a pair of fluted emerald drops, which she can be seen wearing in a photograph with her son, Princie, from about 1948, as well as a pair similar in style to the lotus-flower motif of her necklace. Today, some of her jewelry is in private hands, but the whiff of mystery continues to linger about certain objects, which are still unaccounted for.

Fig. 34. Dragonfly Fairy brooch formerly owned by Barbara Hutton. Paris, France, 1944. Diamonds, rubies, emeralds, platinum. Van Cleef & Arpels' Collection

Power, charisma, beauty—these are the key ingredients for women of great stature,
especially in the figure of Argentinean Eva Péron. She was only twenty-six years old when
she married Colonel Juan Péron, yet her innate smarts and natural connection with the
working class served her well during her brief time as First Lady of Argentina, from 1946
to 1952, when she died at the age of thirty-three from cancer. Evita, as she became known,
may have had the common touch, but she loved finery, especially jewelry, and in this
regard three pieces from Van Cleef & Arpels stand out: a specially commissioned brooch
of the Argentine flag, with Mystery-Set sapphires and white and yellow diamonds;[36] a
jeweled watch set with diamonds, rubies, sapphires, and a hexagonal pattern in gold;[37] and
a multi-strand diamond necklace, worn on formal occasions and a diamond bracelet (figs.
41, 42).

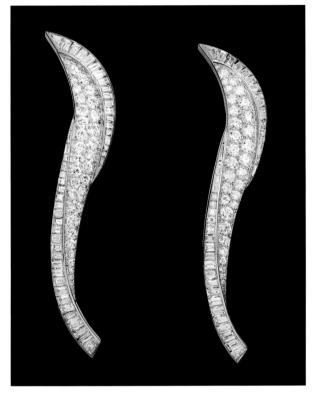

Fig. 36. Flame pair of brooches of the
model owned by Jacqueline Kennedy
Onassis. Paris, France, 1934. Diamonds,
platinum. Van Cleef & Arpels'
Collection

Fig. 37. Poodle brooch of the model
owned by Jacqueline Kennedy
Onassis. Diamonds, rubies, gold. Paris,
France, 1960. Courtesy of a California
Collection

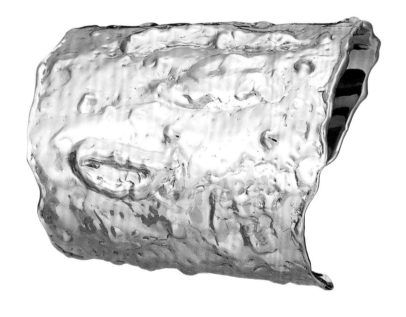

Fig. 38. Etruscan Cuff pair of bracelets
of the model owned by Jacqueline
Kennedy Onassis. Paris, France, 2010.
Gold. Van Cleef & Arpels' Collection

Fig. 39. *Baroda Necklace*. Paris, France,
1951. Gouache on paper. Van Cleef &
Arpels' Archives

Fig. 40a-b. Hindu necklace and pair of earrings formerly owned by the Maharani of Baroda. Paris, France, 1951. Emeralds, diamonds, platinum. Courtesy of Faerber-Collection

Fig. 41. Necklace formerly owned
by Eva Péron. New York, NY, 1949.
Diamonds, platinum. Courtesy of
Private Collection

Fig. 42. Bracelet formerly owned by Eva
Péron. New York, NY, 1949. Diamonds,
platinum. Courtesy of Private
Collection

Fig. 43. Maria Callas signing autographs
following a performance at the Théâtre
des Champs-Elysées, Paris, France,
December 7, 1973. Photo by RDA/Getty
Images

On a far lighter note, and away from the political arena, is a diva of another sort
altogether: the grand Maria Callas (fig. 43). With her proud features and stirring voice,
she was larger than life, and the drama of that life (and lovers, especially Aristotle Onassis,
who purchased jewelry from Van Cleef & Arpels for her) and her operatic career were
catnip for her ever-curious public. When she was dressed in jewelry from Van Cleef &
Arpels, she showed the world that the bejeweled life does not actually require a stage—
just a few exquisite diamonds and glittering stones (fig. 44).

Eva Péron, Maria Callas, Doris Duke, Marjorie Merriweather Post, Grace Kelly, Jacqueline
Kennedy Onassis, Elizabeth Taylor, the Duchess of Windsor—each of these women has
played a critical part in setting style and determining a long-lasting role for the magical
elixir of beauty, dignity, and finery. They have been transformative well beyond their
own lives, and we look to them again and again in matters of taste, temperament, and of
course, jewelry.

Fig. 44. Flower brooch formerly owned
by Maria Callas. Paris, France, 1967.
Platinum, diamonds, rubies. Van Cleef &
Arpels' Collection

Lion ébouriffé (Tousled Lion) brooch owned by H.S.H. Princess Grace of Monaco. Paris, France, 1960. Gold, emeralds, diamonds. Private collection of Her Serene Highness Princess Grace of Monaco, Principality of Monaco

Alhambra pendant on necklace owned by H.S.H. Princess Grace of Monaco. Paris, France, 1973. Yellow gold. Private collection of Her Serene Highness Princess Grace of Monaco, Principality of Monaco

Duck Normandie Brooch Design no. 72873 retail card. Paris, France, 1956. Pigment and ink on card. Van Cleef & Arpels' Archives

Duck brooch owned by H.S.H. Princess Grace of Monaco. Paris, France, 1956. Gold, sapphires, emeralds, diamonds. Private collection of Her Serene Highness Princess Grace of Monaco, Principality of Monaco

Lattice bracelet owned by H.S.H.
Princess Grace of Monaco. Paris, France,
ca. 1935. Diamonds, platinum. Private
Collection of Her Serene Highness
Princess Grace of Monaco, Principality
of Monaco

Pair of earrings of the model owned by
H.S.H. Princess Grace of Monaco. Paris,
France, 1979. Yellow gold, diamonds.
Courtesy of Steven Neckman Inc.

Cascade necklace and pair of earrings.
Paris, France, 1993/1994. Ruby,
diamonds, platinum. This suite was
made for the present owner of the
jarretière formerly owned by Marlene
Dietrich to be worn en suite. Courtesy
of Private Collection, New York

Necklace formed of two *manchette* (cuff) bracelets. Paris, France, 1926 and 1928. Platinum, emeralds, diamonds. Formed by combining two bracelets; formerly owned by Daisy Fellowes. Courtesy of a California Collection

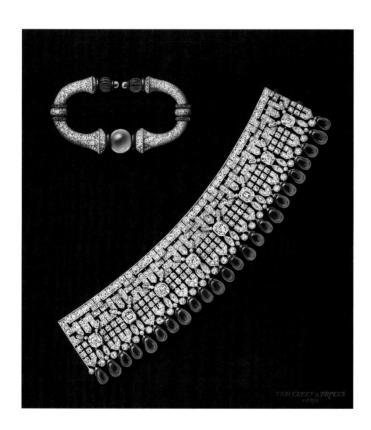

Manchette bracelet catalogue spread. Paris, France, 1925. Printed paper. Van Cleef & Arpels' Archives

Pair of earrings of a model owned
by Jacqueline Kennedy Onassis. Paris,
France, 1970. Yellow gold. Courtesy of
Robin Katz Vintage Jewels

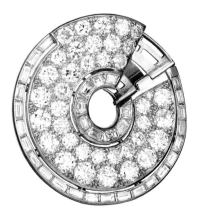
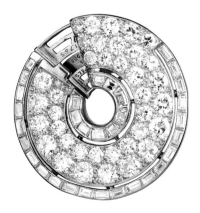

Disc earrings formerly owned by
Barbara Hutton, then Princess Mdivani,
Countess Revenlow. Paris, France,
1934. Diamonds, platinum, yellow gold.
Courtesy of a California Collection

Disc Earrings Design no. 41763 retail
card. Paris, France, 1935. Pigment
and ink on card. Van Cleef & Arpels'
Archives

Eventail earrings formerly owned by
Empress Soraya of Iran. Paris, France,
1950. Diamonds, platinum. Van Cleef &
Arpels' Collection

Mimosa Flowers pair of brooches
formerly owned by Empress Soraya of
Iran. New York, NY, 1948. Yellow gold,
platinum, diamonds. Van Cleef & Arpels'
Collection

Bracelets. Paris, France, ca. 1937.
Gouache on paper. Drawings including
models similar to Paulette Goddard's
Padlock watch (fig. 9) and Natasha
Gelman's Ludo Hexagon bracelet (fig. 18).
Van Cleef & Arpels' Archives

Necklace with detachable clip. Paris,
France, 1946. Diamonds, yellow
gold, platinum. Ordered by Egyptian
Ambassador Bey for Princess
Toussoun of Egypt. Courtesy of
Zendrini Private Collection

NOTES

INNOVATION

1. *History of the New York Athletic Club, Early Years*. The 306' steamer *Varuna* was the largest yacht registered with the New York Athletic Club in 1899. Heir to a carpet business that he sold that year, Higgins also had a house in the south of France. *Varuna*, named for the Hindu god of the ocean, was wrecked off the coast of Madeira in 1909 after hosting some of Europe's monarchy and social elite, including Grand Duke Alexis of Russia. See Amy Dehan, "Tiffany's Buffalo Hunt Cup," in *The Magazine Antiques* (January 2006).
2. Guillaume Apollinaire, *Les peintres cubistes: méditations esthétiques* (Paris: Editions Athéna, 1912).
3. *Encyclopédie des arts décoratifs et industriels modernes au XXème siècle*, section française, PL XXXIX (New York and London, 1977 [reprinted from 1925]).
4. See retail card in VCA archives for 27538 nécessaire.
5. The article written for the 1924 Grand Central Palace exhibition in which VCA exhibited, the Musée Cluny of French medieval art, was cited as a design source for the highest quality of French design.

TRANSFORMATIONS

1. Laura Jacobs provided the information on Louis and Claude Arpels' attendance at Stravinsky's *Firebird* and a later Balanchine production at the Ballets Russes in Paris. Cited in Ruth Peltason, *Living Jewels, Masterpieces from Nature* (New York: The Vendôme Press, 2010): 52.
2. George Balanchine and Frances Mason, *Balanchine's Complete Stories of the Great Ballets* (Garden City, New York: Doubleday, 1977): 347.
3. Interview with Jacqueline Le Henaff, widow of Jean-Marie Le Henaff (1921–2006) and VC&A New York employee (1960–64), August 19, 2010.
4. Interview with Angela Forenza, July 27, 2010.

EXOTICISM

1. French Exposition Corporation, French Exposition of Arts, Commerce, and Industry, "Jewelry and the Orient," in *The French Exposition* (New York, 1924, reprinted by International Studio).
2. The use of the two furnishers is interesting, as both were contracted by VC&A on their own, and both worked with Vladimir Makovsky at times for VC&A and other firms.
3. André Maurois, *"Sur le vif": l'Exposition coloniale* (Paris, 1931).

BEJEWELED LIVES

1. Laura Jacobs, "Grace Kelly's Forever Look," in *Vanity Fair*, May 2010.
2. Grace Kelly had a similar impact on the large Hermès handbag. When she appeared on the cover of *Life* magazine in 1956 holding the bag (in truth, to cover the fact she was pregnant), it started such a craze that the company renamed the accessory the Kelly bag, which it remains to this day.
3. Proddow and Faisel, *Hollywood Jewels*, p. 145.
4. Nadine Brozan, *New York Times*, June 24, 1992.
5. "*Life* Goes to a Party," in *Life* magazine, October 3, 1938.
6. The bracelet was sold at auction by Sotheby's in New York.
7. Although Garbo had other jewelry made by Van Cleef & Arpels, this is the only piece she bought for herself, which she got in 1949, two years before she retired from making films at the age of fifty.
8. Among Goddard's quips: "The only thing you have always to remember: Never, ever sleep with a man until he gives you a pure white stone of at least ten carats," and "I don't accept flowers, I take nothing perishable."
9. Papi and Rhodes, *Famous Jewelry Collectors*, p. 36.
10. The Burtons had homes in Beverly Hills and Gstaad, Switzerland.
11. Van Cleef & Arpels Archives.
12. The society hairdresser Alexandre made a grand hairdo of embedded flowers and jewels for the star, and draped a fringe of the pear-shaped diamonds across her perfectly curved, high forehead.
13. Culme and Rayner, *The Jewels of the Duchess of Windsor*.
14. The Gelmans assembled one of the most important collections of European twentieth-century paintings and sculpture, including works by Balthus, Braque, Derain, Joan Miró, Matisse, and Picasso. Natasha

Gelman, who died in 1998, twelve years after her husband, donated the collection to the Metropolitan Museum of Art, New York, a gift valued at $300 million. Ownership of their collection of Mexican paintings, regarded as one of the country's most prominent, has been locked in a legal battle for years.

15. Beaton, *The Glass of Fashion*, p. 138. Beaton further noted that Fellowes "even wore jewelry with her beach suits."

16. Even when Daisy Fellowes dressed in more unusual ensembles—she was a *mannequin mondain* for Schiaparelli—there remained about her a deliberate pose and artful simplicity.

17. At the time of his death in 1956, Frank Jay Gould reportedly increased his $10 million inheritance ten times over while living in France.

18. At the Goulds' resort Soleil d'Or in Juan-les-Pins, the walls were covered with paintings by French Impressionists and their houseguests over the years included Charlie Chaplin, Elizabeth Taylor, and Paul Getty.

19. "The Magnificent Jewels of Florence Jay Gould, April 11, 1984," Christie's auction catalogue, 1984.

20. Although referred to as a tiara in Sylvie Raulet's book, *Van Cleef & Arpels*, page 95, Post's headwear is sometimes referred to as a diadem. The common distinction is that a diadem is like a band and encircles the head, much like a crown, which is a complete circle. A tiara typically forms a semi-circle.

21. Smithsonian website, www.si.edu. The Marie-Louise Diadem has 1,006 old mine-cut diamonds weighing a total of 700 carats, and seventy-nine Persian turquoise stones weighing 540 carats.

22. Within two more decades, the trio of colors had come to symbolize both the French and American flags. Based on information supplied by Catherine Cariou, Heritage Director, Van Cleef & Arpels, Paris.

23. This tendency of Duke's to reuse family stones was a way of remaining connected to her much happier childhood, principally spent at Duke Farms in New Jersey, a compound of 2,700 acres.

24. The Marquesa de Cuevas, née Margaret Strong, inherited $27 million upon the death of her grandfather, John D. Rockefeller, in 1937.

25. Doris Duke and Porfirio Rubirosa were divorced fourteen months following their marriage in 1947, whereas it was reported in *Life* magazine that Barbara Hutton's marriage to Rubirosa in 1953 lasted seventy-two days. *Life* magazine, March 22, 1954, p. 56.

26. In November 1999, Christie's Geneva auctioned Barbara Hutton's single-strand pearl necklace, which was formerly the property of Marie-Antoinette, Princess of Hungary and Bohemia, Archduchess of Austria, and Queen of France. It was made up of forty-one graduated pearls, measuring approximately 8.50 to 16.35 mm. It was sold for the then world record of $1.45 million. According to *Life* magazine, July 18, 1938, Hutton's debutante party was held at the Ritz in New York at a cost of $60,000.

27. The relationship between Van Cleef & Arpels and the dance world dates back at least to the 1940s. Louis Arpels loved both theatre and ballet, and the great choreographer George Balanchine formed a close relationship with Claude Arpels in New York.

28. Over the course of her relationship with Van Cleef & Arpels, which included the years of her seven marriages, Barbara Hutton purchased as many as three dozen cufflinks. Van Cleef & Arpels Archives.

29. Van Cleef & Arpels Archives.

30. Information about the tiara from Catherine Cariou. By comparison, around this time, Claude Arpels was quoted in the *New York Times* as saying "At Van Cleef & Arpels, where 'tiaras are always in demand,' prices go from $20,000 to $300,000." A more amusing comment was attributed to Mrs. Cornelius Vanderbilt Whitney, who remarked that she wore her tiara—once owned by the Empress of Austria—with "four bobby pins. . . . I enjoy wearing it because it's light and so well distributed. A heavy tiara can ruin a woman's evening.'" Enid Nemy, "From Sultan or Store, Tiaras Can Be Woman's Crowning Glory," in *New York Times*, May 12, 1978, p. 78.

31. The Flame clips are also known as *haricots* because they are shaped somewhat like string beans. Photos from this period show that the First Lady would wear a pair of Flame pins clipped to a triple strand of pearls.

32. Alexandre, who coiffed the First Lady's hair, called the style "Fontanges 1960," a reference to the hair style of the duchesse de Fontanges, a mistress of Louis XIV, some three hundred years earlier. From Bowles, *Jacqueline Kennedy*, p. 129.

33. "La Présidente," in *Time* magazine, June 6, 1961.

34. In 1953, the Maharani of Baroda sold a pair of emerald and diamond anklets to jeweler Harry Winston, who remade them into a fabulous necklace, purchased by the Duchess of Windsor. In 1957, both women happened to be at the same gala where the Duchess was wearing the Winston necklace. The Maharani was heard to exclaim that those same jewels had once been her becoming anklets. The story goes that an outraged and embarrassed Duchess returned the purchase to Harry Winston.

35. *Time* magazine, March 26, 1956.

36. The flag brooch was presented to Eva Péron prior to 1949.

37. The jeweled watch was a cunning blend of the elegant and the practical, especially for this image-conscious politician, because it was actually a secret wristwatch, with the watch face hidden beneath the surface of massed diamonds.

SELECTED BIBLIOGRAPHY

Blum, Dilys E. *Shocking: The Art and Fashion of Elsa Schiaparelli*. Philadelphia: Philadelphia Museum of Art, 2003.

Bowles, Hamish. *Jacqueline Kennedy: The White House Years, Selections from the John F. Kennedy Library and Museum*. New York and Boston: The Metropolitan Museum of Art and Bulfinch Press, 2001.

Culme, John, and Nicholas Rayner. *The Jewels of the Duchess of Windsor*. New York: Vendôme Press in association with Sotheby's, 1987.

Clais, Anne-Marie. *Discovering Van Cleef & Arpels*. Paris: Assouline, 2001.

Gabardi, Melissa. *Les Bijoux de l'Art Deco aux Années 40*. Paris: Editions de l'Amateur, 1986.

Haugland, H. Kristina. *Grace Kelly: Icon of Style to Royal Bride*. New Haven: Yale University Press in association with the Philadelphia Museum of Art, 2006.

"Jewelry and the Orient." In *International Studio*, vol. 79. New York: Offices of the International Studio, 1924. Originally published in French Exposition Corporation, *The French Exposition: Arts, Commerce, and Industries of France and Her Colonies....* New York: French Exposition Corporation, 1924.

Müller, Florence. "Mode." In *Les Années 20*. Paris: Editions du Regard, 1989.

Papi, Stefano, and Alexandra Rhodes. *Famous Jewelry Collectors*. New York: Harry N. Abrams, 1999.

Peltason, Ruth. *Living Jewels: Masterpieces from Nature*. New York: Vendôme Press, 2010.

Petit, Marc. *Van Cleef & Arpels: Reflections of Eternity*. Paris: Editions Cercle d'Art, 2006.

Price, Judith. *Masterpieces of French Jewelry*. London: Running Press, 2006.

Prior, Katherine, and John Adamson. *Maharajas' Jewels*. Paris: Assouline, 2000.

Proddow, Penny, and Debra Healy. *American Jewelry: Glamour and Tradition*. New York: Rizzoli, 1987.

Proddow, Penny, and Marion Fasel. *Diamonds: A Century of Spectacular Jewels*. New York: Harry N. Abrams, 1996.

Proddow, Penny, Debra Healy, and Marion Fasel. *Hollywood Jewels: Movies, Jewelry, Stars*. New York: Harry N. Abrams, 1992.

Raulet, Sylvie. *Art Deco Jewelry*. New York: Rizzoli, 1985.

_____. *Van Cleef & Arpels*. New York: Rizzoli, 1987.

Serres, Michel, Franco Cologni, Jean-Claude Sabrier, and Sharon Kerman. *Van Cleef & Arpels: The Poetry of Time*. Paris: Editions Cercle d'Art, 2009.

Snowman, A. Kenneth. *The Master Jewelers*. New York: Harry N. Abrams, 1990.

Taylor, Elizabeth. *My Love Affair with Jewelry*. New York: Simon & Schuster, 2002.

Train, Susan, ed. *Théâtre de la Mode*. New York: Rizzoli, 1991.

Palais Galliera. *Van Cleef & Arpels*, exh. cat. Paris: Paris-Musées, 1992.

Van Cleef & Arpels. *The Spirit of Beauty*. Paris: Editions Xavier Barral, 2009.

_____. "Van Cleef & Arpels à Galliera." In *L'Estampille, L'Objet d'Art*, no. 5. Dijon: Editions Faton, 1992.

Weber, Christianne. *Art Deco Schmuck*. Munich: Wilhelm Heyne Verlag, 2000.

ARTICLES

Jacobs, Laura. "Grace Kelly's Forever Looks." In *Vanity Fair* (May 2010).

_____. "The Balanchine Tapestries." In *Ballet Review* (Summer 2008), pp. 26–39.

The Magnificent Jewels of Florence J. Gould. New York: Christie's (April 11, 1984).

SELECTED INDEX

Italics denote illustrations.

Aga Khan, 71, 108
Alhambra, 119, 168–69, 171, 208, 229, 230, 234, *234, 272*
Arpels, Charles, 13, 192
Arpels, Claude, 41, 94, 97, 103, 246, 248, 263, 281
Arpels, Hélène, *124*, 193, 195, *195*
Arpels, Jacques, 41, 263
Arpels, Louis, 37, 41, 94, 97, 193, 236, 246, 281
Art Deco, 14, 17, 18, 24, 41, 50, *51*, 101, 149, 164, *191*, 193, *194*, 204, 209, *210, 214, 224*, 229, 243, *245*, 246, 248, 249, *258*
Art Nouveau, 12, 13, 14, 111, 164

Baker, Josephine, 164
Balanchine, George, 94, 97, 280, 281
Balenciaga, Cristobal, 201
Ballets Russes, 17, 94, 156
Baroda, Maharani of (née Sita Devi), 85, *87*, 152, 263, *266–67*, 281
Baroda, Pratapsinghrao Gaewad, Maharajah of, 263
Bing, Samuel, 12
Black, Starr, and Frost, 24
Blue Heart diamond, 254
Burton, Richard, 240, 243, 280

Callas, Maria, 254, *270, 271*
Chanel, Gabrielle "Coco," 197
Chaplin, Charlie, 239, 281
Cocteau, Jean, 248
Castellane, Comtesse de (née Anna Gould), 258
Coward, Noel, 259
Cromwell, James, 256, *256*

Cuervas, Marquesa de (née Margaret Strong), 258, *258*
Cunard, Nancy, 197

Dalí, Salvador, 198, 248
Delaunay, Robert, 17
Delaunay, Sonia, 17
Deneuve, Catherine, *227*
Dietrich, Marlene, 8, 234, 236, *236–37*, 238, *274*
Disney, 98, 111
Duke, Doris, 31, 254, 256, *256*, 259, 261, 270, 281
Dunand, Jean, 17, 158, *160*
Duvalet, Maurice, 101

Eugénie, Empress, 85, *87*

Fabergé, Karl, 12, 13, 249
Fakhry, Mahmoud, Pacha of Egypt, 254
Farrells, Suzanne, 97
Farouk, King, 259
Fellowes, Daisy, 73, 195, 197, 246, *250–51, 275*, 281
Flynn, Errol, 256
Forenza, Angela, 103, 280
Frank, Jean-Michel, 17

Garbo, Greta, 8, 234, 238, *238*, 280
Gelman, Jacques, 243, 280
Gelman, Natasha Zakalkowa, 243, *248, 249, 278*, 280
Gide, André, 248
Goddard, Paulette, 31, *226*, 239, *239, 278*, 280
Gould, Florence Jay (La Caze), 26, 192, 248, 249, *252*, 261, 281
Gould, Frank Jay, 192, 248, 281
Grant, Cary, 230, 259

Harry Winston, 254, 281
Higgins, Eugene, 11, *12*, 280
House of Worth, 193
Hutton, Barbara, 259, *259*, 260, 261, *263, 276*, 281

Kahlo, Frida, 243
Kelly, Grace, *see* Monaco, H.S.H. Princess Grace of
Kennedy Onassis, Jacqueline, First Lady, 8, 261, *264–65*, 270, *276*, 281
Kennedy, John F., President, 261

Camargo, La, 85, *88–89*
Lacaze, René-Sim, 32, 199, *247*, 256
Lalique, René, 12, 13, 14
Lancret, Nicolas, 85, *88*
Langlois, Alfred, 24, 26, 41, 101
Lanvin, Jeanne, 198
Le Henaff, Jean-Louis, 101, 280
Le Henaff, Jean-Marie, 101, 280
Leleu, Jules, 17
Ludo bracelet, 37, *38–39*, 197, 199, 229, 243, 246, *249*, 256, *260–61, 278*

Makovsky, Vladimir, 24, 280
Marie-Antoinette, 259, 281
Marlborough, Duchess of (née Consuelo Vanderbilt), *258*
Minaudière, 26, 28, 30, 37, *44–45*, 73, *87*, 192, *193*, 204, 229, 248, 261
Monaco, H.S.H. Prince Rainier of, 230, *230*
Monaco, H.S.H. Princess Grace of, *back cover, 2*, 8, 229–30, *230–33*, 234, *234, 235*, 270, *272, 273*, 280
Monaco, Princess Caroline of, 234, *235*

Mystery Setting, *cover*, 8, *10*, 28, 30, 31, *33*, *34*, 37, *60*, 111, 115, *126–27*, 198, *221*, 229, 243, *245*, 254, *255*, 264

Onassis, Aristotle, 261, 270

Patton, George, General, 256
Patou, Jean, 17, 195
Péron, Eva, a.k.a., "Evita," 264, *268–69*, 270
Péron, Juan, Colonel, 264
Piaget, 103
place Vendôme, 13, 41, 73, 85, *86*, *90*, *105*, *106*, 246
Post, Marjorie Merriweather, 249, 253, *253*, 254, *254*, *255*, 259, 270, 281
Caroline, Princess of Monaco, 234, *234*

Rainier III, Prince of Monaco, 230, *230*
Redon, Odilon, 13
Richemont, 103
Rivera, Diego, 243, *248*
Rouff, Maggie, 198, 200
Rubel, John (Jean), 101
Rubirosa, Porfirio, 256, 259, 281
Ruhlmann, Jean-Jacques, 17

Schiaparelli, Elsa, 197, 199, 200, 281
Sirikit, Queen of Thailand, 41, 168, 204
Smithsonian Institution, 253, 254, 281
Strauss, Allard, Meyer, 18, 24, 156
Soraya, Empress of Iran, *277*
Symbolism, 13
Swanson, Gloria, 234

Taylor, Elizabeth, Dame, 8, 240, *240–42*, 243, *244–45*, 270, 281
Tiffany & Co., 24, 103
Tiffany, Louis Comfort, 12, 14, 280
Toussoun, Princess of Egypt, *279*

Van Cleef, Alfred, 13
Van Cleef, Estelle, 13, 28
Vionnet, Madeleine, 198
Vladimir, Grand Duchess, 259

Walska, Ganna, *70*, 73, *86*
Windsor, Duchess of (Wallis Warfield Simpson), 8, 32, 164, 199, 243, *247*, 254, 270, 280, 281
Windsor, Duke of, a.k.a. King Edward VIII of England, 199, 243, *246*
Winterhalter, Franz-Xaver, 85, *87*

Zip necklace, 32, 36, 71, 73, *76–77*, 204, 229

ACKNOWLEDGMENTS

Cooper-Hewitt, National Design Museum is particularly grateful to the following individuals and organizations for their assistance and support during the preparation of the *Set in Style: The Jewelry of Van Cleef & Arpels* exhibition and catalogue.

Sarah Atkins
Artists Rights Society: Andrea Fisher
Claude Arpels
John Arpels
Kate Becker
Barbara Berkowitz
Larry Bishop
William Boyes
Maria Bussman
Iris Cantor
Christie's: Francesco Alvera,
    Libby Dale, Daphne Lingon
Lucille Coleman
Condé Nast Publications:
    Katie Dixon, Georgie Fletcher
Corbis Images: Oscar Espaillat
M. Elaine Crocker
Ivette Dabah
Dallas Museum of Art:
    Martha McLeod
Doris Duke Charitable Foundation:
    Kate Holland
Duke University Archives,
    Doris Duke Collection:
    Mary Samouelian
Katharina Faerber
Thomas Faerber
Tony Falcone
Marianne Fisher
Angela Forenza
Elliot Friman
Susan Gale
Getty Images: Sondra Zaharias
Elizabeth Hada
Tino Hammid
Susan Hermanos
Hillwood Estate Museum and

Gardens: Liana Paredes,
    Gina Raimond
Carolyn Hsu-Balcer
John Fitzgerald Kennedy Library:
    Maryrose Grossman
Wendy Kaplan
Robin Katz
Carolyn Kelly
Peter Kjaer
Dr. Katie Klehr
Jonathan Kleinhaus
Miriam Knapp
Sylvia Kuttner
Neil Lane
Jacqueline Le Henaff
Peter van Lennep
Dr. Joseph and Mrs. Karen Levine
Audrey Friedman and
    Haim Manishevitz
David Massey
Erin McCluskey
Dennis Meyers
Tim Mendelson
Yi Ming
Principality of Monaco: Hervé Irien,
    Carl de Lencquesaing
Karyn Murphy
Steven Neckman
Perseus Books: Bill Jones
Craig Reisfield
Richemont: Scott Barefoot
Stefan Richter
Barbara Roan
Gaetan Rousseau
Hazel Shanken
Jean S. and Frederic A. Sharf
Lee Siegelson
Lacy Simkowitz
Sotheby's: Carol Elkins,
    Antonio Fragoso, Lisa Hubbard,
    Victoria de la Soujeole,
    Emily Waterfall
Sotheby's Picture Library–Cecil
    Beaton Studio Archive:
    Katherine Marshall
Pauline Sugino

Dorothea Swope
Dame Elizabeth Taylor
John Bigelow Taylor
Suzanne Tennenbaum
Martin Travis
University of Texas at Austin,
    Fine Arts Library: Karen Holt
Nishan Vartanian
Jay Waldman
The Wallace Collection:
    Nell Carrington
Micah Walters
Carlo Zendrini
Cristina Monet-Palaci Zilkha
Chris Zill
and all Anonymous Lenders

At Van Cleef & Arpels International:
    Dominique Fumée,
    Jean Bienayme, Sibylle Jammes,
    Frédéric Gilbert-Zinck,
    Isabelle Godard, Antoine Lacroix,
    Claire Masquelier,
    Jean-Jacques Masson,
    Laetitia Abdelli,
    Frédéric Morales, Solène Taquet,
    Cynthia Crozat, Caroline Trappler
At Van Cleef & Arpels USA:
    Cindy Prasnal, Diana Bernal,
    Alvina Patel, Angel Chen,
    Catherine Harrison, Inezita Gay,
    Astrid de Place, Helen King,
    Christiane Ouvrier, Patrice Levrat

At Cooper-Hewitt:
Communications and Marketing:
    Jennifer Northrop,
    Laurie Olivieri
Conservation: Perry Choe,
    Annie Hall
Curatorial: Cara McCarty,
    Matilda McQuaid,
    Gregory Herringshaw,
    Cynthia Trope
Development and External Affairs:
    Sophia Amaro, Kate Dobie,

Kelly Mullaney
Education: Caroline Payson,
    Shamus Adams,
    Kimberly Cisneros, Mei Mah
Exhibitions: Jocelyn Groom,
    Matthew O'Connor,
    Mathew Weaver
Finance: Christopher Jeannopoulos
IT: Jimpson Pell, Elvis Reyes
OFEO: Janice Slivko
OPS: James Kirk, John Talkington
Publications: Chul R. Kim
Registrar: Steven Langehough,
    Melanie Fox, Wendy Rogers,
    Bethany Romanowski,
    Larry Silver
Interns: Susheela Goli,
    Adriana Kertzer,
    Cordelia Lembo, Sarah Richter,
    Danielle Sonnekalb, Sara Vincent

Smithsonian Institution:
    Jennifer Kroan, Richard Kurin,
    Daniel Paisley, Jeffrey Post

Design Team:
Installation design: Jouin/Manku:
    Patrick Jouin, Elodie Martin;
    Echelle 1: Alain Szabason,
    Loic Thoré
Exhibition graphics and book
    design: Tsang Seymour Design:
    Catarina Tsang, Patrick Seymour,
    Elena Penny, Marine Thebault,
    Jueun Cho
iPad app design: 2x4, Inc.:
    Georgie Stout,
    Douglas Freedman,
    Jonathan Lee, Kostadin Krajcev
Lighting design:
    L'Observatoire International
Electrical engineering:
    AKF Engineers

PHOTOGRAPHIC CREDITS

TITLE PAGE: photo: Tino Hammid, © California Collection. CONTENTS: photo: Tino Hammid, © California Collection. FOREWORD: photo: Patrick Gries, © Van Cleef & Arpels. INNOVATION: photo: Patrick Gries, © Van Cleef & Arpels: p. 10, figs. 1, 4–9, 11, 13, 14, 16, 18–21, 23, 38; pp. 44–48, 50, 51, 53-57, 59, 64-67, 69. Photo: Matt Flynn, © Smithsonian Institution: figs. 2, 12, 17, 29. © Van Cleef & Arpels: figs. 10, 15, 22, 25, 32, 36, 37; pp. 53, 56, 61. Photo: Tony Falcone, © Christie's Images Ltd.: fig. 24. © David Massey: figs. 26, 28. Photo: Tony Falcone, © Private Collection, Chicago: fig. 27; pp. 52, 60, 65. Photo: Patrick Gries, © Private Collection: fig. 3. Photo: Tony Falcone, © Private Collection: fig. 31; pp. 48, 60, 62, 68. Photo: Tony Falcone, © Cristina Monet-Palaci Zilkha: fig. 34. Photo: Tino Hammid, © California Collection: figs. 30, 33; pp. 45, 52, 55, 62, 64; Photo: Tino Hammid, © Collection of Neil Lane: fig. 35; pp. 47, 52; © Sotheby's: p. 49. Photo: Rish Durka, © Symbolic & Chase: p. 58. Photo: Denis Hayoun/Diode SA, © Christie's Images Ltd.: p. 59. Photo: Tony Falcone, © Jean S. and Frederic A. Sharf: pp. 62, 63. Photo: David Behl, © Primavera Gallery, New York: p. 63. TRANSFORMATIONS: photo: Patrick Gries, © Van Cleef & Arpels: 14a, 1–4, 9,10, 16, 21a,b–25, 27, 29, 30, 31, 36–39, 41–43; pp. 105, 106. Photo: Tino Hammid, © California Collection: 5a–c, 6a,b, 12, 15, 26a,b; p. 104. © Van Cleef & Arpels: figs. 7, 13, 18, 20, 28, 34, 107. Photo: Tony Falcone, © Jean S. and Frederic A. Sharf: fig. 8; pp. 105, 107. Photo: Tony Falcone, © Waldmann, Inc.: fig. 11. Photo: Gaetan Rousseau, © Van Cleef & Arpels: fig. 14b. © The Trustees of the Wallace Collection, London: fig. 17. © Sotheby's: fig. 19. © Primavera Gallery, New York: fig. 32. Photo: Tony Falcone, © Private Collection: fig. 33; pp. 104, 108. Photo: Tony Falcone, © Vartanian & Sons, Inc.: fig. 35; p. 108. Photo: Tino Hammid, © Collection of Neil Lane: fig. 40. Photo: Tony Falcone, © Private Collection, New York: p. 106. Photo: Rish Durka, © Symbolic & Chase: p. 109. NATURE AS INSPIRATION: photo: Tony Falcone, © Jean S. and Frederic A. Sharf: p. 110. Photo: Patrick Gries, © Van Cleef & Arpels: 1, 3, 4, 6, 8, 11, 13–15, 25, 26, 29, 31, 33–35, 37, 43; pp. 138–43. Photo: Guy Lucas de Peslouan, © Van Cleef & Arpels: fig. 2. © Van Cleef & Arpels: figs. 5, 10, 23, 24, 42; pp. 144–47. © Sotheby's: fig. 7. Photo: Tony Falcone, © Private Collection: figs. 9, 12, 17–20, 32;

p. 145. Photo: Tino Hammid, © Collection of Neil Lane: fig. 16. Photo: Tony Falcone, © Vartanian & Sons, Inc.: fig. 21. Photo: Tony Falcone, © Jean S. and Frederic A. Sharf: figs. 22, 41. Photo: Tino Hammid, © California Collection: figs. 27, 28, 38–40. Photo: Tony Falcone, © Private Collection, Chicago: fig. 30; pp. 142, 144, 145. Photo: Patrick Gries, © Susan Gale: fig. 36. EXOTICISM: photo: Patrick Gries, © Van Cleef & Arpels: figs. 1–4, 7, 11, 15–21, 23, 25–27, 29–31, 33, 34; pp. 148, 183, 184, 185, 187–89. Photo: Tony Falcone, © Christie's Images Ltd.: figs. 5a,b. © Van Cleef & Arpels: figs. 6, 8, 12, 22; pp. 184–86. Photo: Tino Hammid, © California Collection: fig. 9. Photo: Andrew Garn, © Smithsonian Institution: fig. 10. Photo: Tony Falcone, © Private Collection: figs. 13, 14, 28. Photo: Lucien Capehart Photography, Inc., © Richters of Palm Beach: fig. 24. Photo: Matt Flynn, © Smithsonian Institution: fig. 32. © Sotheby's: p. 182. Photo: Tony Falcone, © Carolyn Hsu-Balcer: p. 186. MENKES: Photo: Patrick Gries, © Van Cleef & Arpels: figs. 1, 4, 6, 8–11, 13–15, 17, 19, 21–25, 27, 28; pp. 190, 214–19, 221–66. © Van Cleef & Arpels: figs. 2, 3, 5, 7, 18, 20, 220, 225–27. Photo: Tony Falcone, © Private Collection: fig. 12; pp. 211, 225. Photo: Tony Falcone, © Vartanian & Sons, Inc.: fig. 16. Photo: Tony Falcone, © Van Cleef & Arpels: p. 213. Photo: Tino Hammid, © Collection of Neil Lane: p. 219. PELTASON: © H.S.H. Princess Grace of Monaco, Principality of Monaco: figs. 3a–d; pp. 228, 272, 273. © Van Cleef & Arpels: figs. 2, 10, 16, 20, 33, 39; pp. 272, 275, 276, 278. © Estate of Yousuf Karsh: fig. 3. Photo: Patrick Gries, © Van Cleef & Arpels: figs. 4, 5, 6, 8, 9, 15, 18, 2–23, 29, 30, 32, 34, 36, 38, 44; pp. 274–77. © Picture Post/Hulton Archives/Getty Images: fig. 7. Photo: John Bigelow Taylor, © Dame Elizabeth Taylor: figs. 11a,b, 13, 14. Photo: Cecil Beaton/Vogue, © The Condé Nast Publications. Photo: Tino Hammid, © California Collection: fig. 37. © Katharina Faerber: fig. 40a-b

SET IN STYLE: THE JEWELRY OF VAN CLEEF & ARPELS
Sarah D. Coffin with contributions by Suzy Menkes and Ruth Peltason
© 2011 Smithsonian Institution

Published by
Cooper-Hewitt, National Design Museum
Smithsonian Institution
2 East 91st Street
New York, NY 10128, USA
www.cooperhewitt.org

Published on the occasion of the exhibition
Set in Style: The Jewelry of Van Cleef & Arpels
at Cooper-Hewitt, National Design Museum, Smithsonian Institution,
February 18–June 5, 2011.

Set in Style: The Jewelry of Van Cleef & Arpels is made possible by

Van Cleef & Arpels

Additional support is provided by Sofitel Luxury Hotels.

Media sponsorship is provided by NEW YORK

This publication is made possible in part by The Andrew W. Mellon Foundation.

Distributed to the trade in North America by Distributed Art Publishers
155 Sixth Avenue, 2nd floor
New York, NY 10013, USA
www.artbook.com

Published outside North America by Thames & Hudson Ltd.
www.thamesandhudson.com

First edition: February 2011

ISBN: 978-0-910503-85-3 (hardcover)
       978-0-910503-86-0 (paperback)

Museum Editor: Chul R. Kim, Director of Publications

Design: Tsang Seymour Design

Printed in South Korea by Taeshin Inpack Co. Ltd.

Library of Congress Cataloging-in-Publication Data

Coffin, Sarah D.
     Set in Style : The Jewelry of Van Cleef & Arpels / By Sarah D. Coffin et al.
         pages cm
     "Published on the occasion of the exhibition Set in Style: The Jewelry of Van
Cleef & Arpels at Cooper-Hewitt, National Design Museum, Smithsonian Institution,
February 18-June 5, 2011."
     Includes bibliographical references and index.
     ISBN 978-0-910503-85-3 (hardcover : alk. paper) — ISBN 978-0-910503-84-6
(pbk. : alk. paper) 1. Van Cleef & Arpels--Exhibitions. I. Cooper-Hewitt, National
Design Museum, Smithsonian Institution. II. Title.
     NK7398.V36A4 2010
     739.27092'2--dc22
                                      2010048875